Praise for
UNBUNDLING THE ENTERPRISE

"To find novel value (digital treasure), CIOs must dive deep, beyond the surface of websites, and connect the dots in this ever-evolving network of possibilities. *Unbundling the Enterprise* will help you navigate these vast digital seas."

—**Esat Sezer,** cofounder of Ritmus, former CIO of Coca-Cola

"I recommend this book for business folks looking for the 'aha' moment on APIs, and who want to make the business case for APIs in their organization."

—**Mark O'Neill,** Gartner Chief of Research for Software Engineering

"A phenomenal read! Stephen and Matt captivate you from the start. This book will challenge you to re-evaluate your perspective on how you can differentiate yourself in the modern data ecosystem."

—**Jason Beyer,** VP Data & Analytics, Bridgestone

"It's no accident that Stephen and Matt have written a book that clearly lays out a path for success in the digital economy. For years, they have been helping organizations drive new business value through the use of APIs. Not only do they show why the world's most innovative companies have a knack for creating repeatable digital success, but they also identify patterns that every business can emulate to reach their goals."

—**Steve Lucas,** Chairman & CEO of Boomi, author of *Engage to Win*

"In an age where the pace of change is faster than ever, this book offers a road map for leaders to harness the power of digital transformation, bridging the gap between high-level strategy and day-to-day operations. It's about creating a resilient organization that thrives on innovation, ready for the future's challenges and opportunities."

—**John Rowell,** cofounder and CEO, Revenium

"Unbundling the Enterprise provides a blueprint for leveraging APIs to not only achieve seamless integration and enhanced flexibility but also to foster an ecosystem of innovation that can significantly amplify your market reach and financial outcomes."

—**John D'Emic,** cofounder and CTO, Revenium

"Unbundling the Enterprise speaks to the imperative of digital data strategy for exponential value creation. Written in an approachable and easy-to-understand detail, it is an essential guideline for non-technical business leaders and executives responsible for growth."

—**J. Ignacio Puente,** CEO, Ulity, and VP Digital Transformation, Mobility & Subscription Platforms, Global Business Strategy & Operations, Santander

"Fishman and McLarty make an undeniable argument for making more intentional choices today that open a whole world of possibilities tomorrow. The value dynamics chapter alone is worth the price of admission, but I think readers across business, design, and technology will see the wisdom in these pages and find new ways to collaborate, strategize, and win together."

—**Patrick Quattlebaum,** CEO, Harmonic Design and coauthor of *Orchestrating Experiences*

"With powerful, real-world examples drawn from both digital disruptors and well-established incumbent firms in a variety of industries, *Unbundling the Enterprise* is an essential read for leaders striving to build an antifragile, thriving business poised for sustainable growth."

—**Mahesh Motiramani,** Head of Enterprise Customer Success, Workato

"I reckon this book will be on the desk of all digital leaders and aspirants soon. The new math weaves optionality, opportunity, and optimization beautifully. While value dynamics is a powerful technique, the economic framing of APIs through the lens of optionality is refreshing."

—**Dinkar Gupta,** Chief Information and Technology Officer, KPMG Switzerland

Stephen Fishman   Matt McLarty

UNBUNDLING THE ENTERPRISE

—

APIs, Optionality & the Science of Happy Accidents

IT Revolution
Independent Publisher Since 2013
Portland, Oregon

25 NW 23rd Pl, Suite 6314
Portland, OR 97210

First Edition
Printed in the United States of America
28 27 26 25 24   1 2 3 4 5 6 7 8 9

Cover design by Julianna Johnson and Kate Giambrone, Bologna Sandwich LLC.
Book design and illustrations by Devon Smith Creative LLC.

Library of Congress Cataloging-in-Publication Data
Names: Fishman, Stephen, author. | McLarty, Matt, author.
Title: Unbundling the enterprise : APIs, optionality, and the science of happy accidents /
Stephen Fishman & Matt McLarty.
Description: Portland, OR : IT Revolution, [2024] | Includes bibliographical references.
Identifiers: LCCN 2024011612 (print) | LCCN 2024011613 (ebook) | ISBN 9781950508877
(paperback) | ISBN 9781950508884 (ebook) | ISBN 9781950508891 (pdf) | ISBN 9781950508907
Subjects: LCSH: Business--Technological innovations. | Application program interfaces
(Computer software) | BISAC: COMPUTERS / Internet / Web Services & APIs |
BUSINESS & ECONOMICS / Leadership
Classification: LCC HF5548.2 .F475 2024 (print) | LCC HF5548.2 (ebook) |
DDC 658/.0553--dc23/eng/20240514
LC record available at https://lccn.loc.gov/2024011612
LC ebook record available at https://lccn.loc.gov/2024011613

ISBN: 9781950508877
eBook ISBN: 9781950508884
Web PDF ISBN: 9781950508891
Audiobook ISBN: 9781950508907

For information about special discounts for bulk purchases
or for information on booking authors for an event, please visit our website at
www.ITRevolution.com.

Dedication

Stephen—To my amazing wife, Kathleen Kelly, who inspired me to find my voice and made it possible for me to be of service to the world around me. To my parents, who helped me get a world-class education. To my children, Marina and Abigail, for making me a better person. And to my many friends and colleagues who helped me develop into a professional contributor and leader with something to offer the community.

Matt—For Chris, for her patience, for her support, for her love. For Daniel and Josiah, for reminding me what's important in life.

Contents

List of Figures

Prologue

Astounding Pirate Innovation

The Dread Pirate Greybeard stands at the helm of his famous ship, *The Legacy*. He steadies its course with his right hand. In his left, he clutches a rolled-up piece of paper: a treasure map. It took three years to track down the map, another year to hire the temperamental but uniquely skilled crew, and then the better part of another year to pack the ship and make it seaworthy. For the last month, they have sailed the treacherous seas. But finally—finally!—they see it. "Land ho!" yells a deckhand from the crow's nest. After executing their meticulous plan for five long years, they have made it to Treasure Island.

Two crew members drop anchor while the rest load rowboats with supplies: picks, shovels, and ropes. In the blink of an eye, the motley crew of pirates thrash their oars with excitement as a procession of rowboats makes its way to shore. The group forms two lines on the beach as the final boat arrives, carrying their fearless leader triumphantly to dry land. "Treasure!" he shouts, holding the map in the air. "Like I promised ye five years ago, there's no other option: with this, we'll all be rich!" The crew explodes in shouts of excitement and celebration.

Greybeard consults the map and then marches impatiently toward a distant rock. "The first marker," he mutters, his pirate crew in tow. From there, they venture through jungles, over quicksand, and under the shadow of a volcano until they finally reach a clearing with a shimmering lagoon. "We're close," Greybeard sputters. "I can almost taste it." Consulting the map, he makes his way to a lone palm tree. Slowly and carefully, he takes ten measured paces to his left. Turning to his right, he takes twenty paces forward, bringing him to the edge of the lagoon. With a final turn to his left, he crawls the last twelve paces, his nose almost touching the sand. He stops suddenly, eyes bulging from his weathered face. The crew rushes to his side, desperate to see what has frozen their fearless leader. There, only slightly covered in sand, is an iron cross. Greybeard rotates it slightly so everyone can see it. *X* marks the spot!

"Dig, me hearties! DIG!" shouts Greybeard. Picks and shovels rain down on the area. Sand flies in all directions. Soon, the crew reaches clay, but nothing can slow their furious excavation. Within minutes, they are three feet beneath the ground. After a quarter of an hour, they've almost dug a lagoon of their own. "Keep digging!" says Greybeard with a slight quiver. "It's here. I know it. The map got us this far. It can't be wrong!" But hours more of digging doesn't turn up any treasure. Only the bones of those who had dug before. Demoralized, Greybeard and his crew retreat to their ship at sundown.

In the morning, Greybeard and his crew awaken to an unusual sight. Beached on the island is a pirate ship the likes of which they have never seen. The Jolly Roger flies from its main mast, but this vessel appears to be a collection of rafts roped together, wider than ten pirate ships combined, and completely covered in wooden crates. The puzzled pirates look on as a masked, black-clad figure emerges from the center of the super raft. "Good morning!" shouts the stranger. "The name's Bob. Fine morning for a treasure hunt, wouldn't you say?"

With that, the stranger tears a side off the first crate, letting its jangling contents spill onto the beach. From *The Legacy*, it's impossible to tell what the contraptions are that fall from the crate, but the crew sees Captain Bob pick one up and start winding it with a metal key. He puts the device down, and it scurries across the beach, stopping a hundred or so yards away. It starts digging furiously, creating a miniature sandstorm. Bob winds another device, then another, until all the devices have scurried to seemingly random spots on the island, digging relentlessly once they arrive. He repeats the process with every crate until it appears the whole island is covered with these mechanical pirates. Captain Bob walks casually toward his innumerable, unliving crew, surveying their handiwork.

DING! A loud bell rings out from behind a distant dune. Bob rushes toward the sound. "Aha!" he screams. "Long John's silver! I thought it might be here." DONG! A bell rings farther inland. "Whoa! I've never seen so many pearls in my life!" GONG! Farther still. "By Davy Jones's locker, it's the lost gold of Montezuma!" On board *The Legacy*, the crew stands silently, jaws agape as they watch a parade of treasure return to the raft, carried by a mischief of clockwork mice. Greybeard tears his map to shreds, then slowly throws its pieces one by one into the sea…

Introduction

There's treasure out there in the digital seas! But figuring out how to find it requires a deep understanding of the digital business landscape—both its opportunities and its obstacles. Since the World Wide Web took hold three decades ago, enterprises established before the dawn of the web have been trying to figure out how to navigate the new landscape and how they can map it to find digital treasure. These *digital settlers* have tried to apply the best practices of pre-web business, such as five-year plans and linear production lines, to their digital delivery but have yielded limited returns. Moving a large organization away from its status quo is hard, but establishing an effective new operating model is impossible if you don't understand the paradigm in which you are working. This is why so many established organizations have struggled with digital transformation.

Within that same thirty-year period, a new generation of web-native companies was born. These startups had no existing practices to apply to digital business. They were new companies aware that they were playing a new game. As opposed to viewing the web as a new channel to be added to their operating model, these *digital pirates* embraced the properties of the web as the essence of their business models: data as the raw material for creating digital products; high-speed, low-cost communication; and mass observability. Whether by necessity or design, these web startups were defining a new methodology for digital treasure hunting.

People first understood the web to be a collection of websites. Most companies—the digital settlers—moved quickly to create home pages that their customers could visit. But the digital pirates saw the web differently. Looking beneath the surface of the browser, they saw the internet as a way to easily and cheaply connect businesses to each other. Visionaries like Tim O'Reilly imagined the web as a network of digital services that any company could access. Early believers in this vision, like eBay and Amazon, made it a reality by creating APIs (application programming interfaces) for their digital products and services.

In the simplest terms, an API is an interface that allows software to talk to other software over the web. Unlike a GUI (graphical user interface), which is optimized to be used by humans, an API is optimized to be used by software programs. Developers create APIs/interfaces to deliver software functionality and data to other software programs (software-based consumers). Other organizations can then build software that accesses the API via network communication. As more companies published APIs on the web, and even more companies started using them, the vision of the web as a digital business ecosystem became real.

To understand how APIs power web experiences, consider a rideshare scenario involving two people: a rider and a driver. The rider orders a ride to the movies on their CloudCo smart speaker, checks the driver location and pickup time on their RideCo app, and then pays for the ride through the app when they reach the theater. The driver accepts the ride request through the RideCo app, locates the rider, and then follows the app's navigation to the destination. The list below illustrates what happens to enable these two user experiences, with APIs playing a big role (see also Figure 0.1).

1. The smart speaker sends the ride request message to CloudCo's backend services using an API.
2. The CloudCo backend then sends the message to RideCo's API.
3. The RideCo driver receives the ride request on their mobile phone via another API.
4. The rider and driver location services are enabled on the RideCo app by connecting to MapCo's geolocation API.

5. RideCo allows the driver and rider to contact one another through the mobile app, which is enabled by TelCo's communications API.

6. Finally, payment services are enabled on the RideCo app with the help of PayCo's payments API.

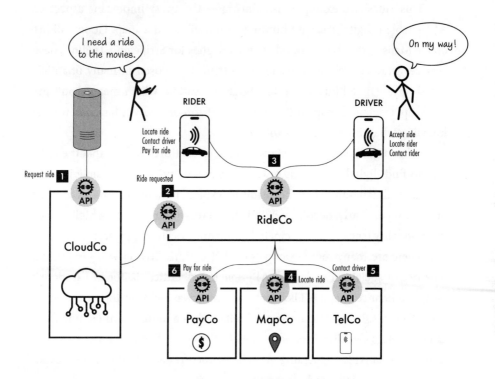

FIGURE 0.1: The Role of APIs in a Rideshare Scenario

The rider has a smooth customer experience, blissfully unaware that they just conducted business with five different companies (six if you count the driver as an independent contractor).

Not only does this example show the role APIs play in powering current digital experiences, but it also shows how a collection of API-enabled services allowed companies like Uber and Lyft to launch and scale in record time. Before the web and APIs, a company wanting to offer transportation services would need to create or buy its own payment software, mapping data, and telecommunications services. With commercially available APIs like Stripe, Google Maps, and Twilio, those capabilities are instantly available. On top of that, both rideshare startups are able to run their applications through API-enabled cloud services, another variable that fueled the rideshare companies' fast start and rapid growth.

This rideshare example also illustrates the most important aspect of API-enabled digital treasure hunting: you don't need a map. Google didn't create Maps with Uber in mind. The same goes for Stripe and Twilio. These services were created as APIs, allowing them to be used in many unanticipated ways. Digital business is all about innovation, which means you can't draw up a detailed map to the treasures of tomorrow. We have no way of knowing what those treasures will be.

What digital pirates have shown over the last thirty years is that the right way to find digital treasure is to create as many options as possible in your digital landscape and then be ready to exploit new opportunities as they arise—prepare early, decide late. APIs help create options, and a high degree of optionality leads to unanticipated opportunities. To happy accidents.

There are many more examples of API options driving web innovation. The rise of social networks was API-enabled. A critical factor in Facebook's early dominance was its "Like" button, which was built on top of the Facebook Graph API.[1] Mobile apps were built on data and functions coming from cloud services via APIs. Even today's AI (artificial intelligence) boom is largely dependent on APIs. Generative AI is being incorporated into customer experiences through APIs, and corporations are embedding their own services into third-party models via API. All this API-enabled innovation begs the question: Are these digital pirates using some grand design or simply following their intuition?

Whether intentional or not, the good news is that there is a recipe for winning with APIs in the digital economy. This is the book that defines it and makes it accessible for legacy enterprises, the digital settlers.

- In this book, you will learn some of the most illustrative success stories of the digital age, including digital settlers that have successfully transformed.

- You will learn the common methods used by successful organizations: unbundling digital business capabilities, designing digital business models through value exchange, and establishing widespread feedback loops.
- And you will see how those methods can be applied in specific strategies for your business, from optimizing digital channels to amalgamating value streams.

In all these areas, APIs feature prominently.

Treasure-Hunting Methods

The management and strategic practices of the twentieth century can only go so far in the digital economy of the twenty-first century. The most successful digital companies are utilizing methods tailored to the unique challenges and opportunities of the digital age.

Create Optionality Through Unbundling

The digital economy moves at breakneck speed. Innovation happens across all industries and all technical areas. New techniques are combined, leading to further innovations. The result is a business landscape that is as unpredictable as it is full of opportunities. Successful digital companies handle this pace by spending less time trying to predict the future and more time preparing for any eventuality.

Preparation comes in the form of optionality: unbundling their business capabilities into digital assets that can be combined and composed into new products, processes, and experiences that meet opportunities unlocked by innovation. These digital pirates accomplish this by creating APIs for reusable software functions and data that may be used in many different contexts. They also make these APIs as easy to discover and use as possible. This book will show you how to drive optionality in your business using APIs.

Identify Opportunities Through Value Dynamics

Business can be viewed on a macro level as a series of value exchanges (Clayton Christensen's term for the interconnected set of stakeholders that deliver value-producing products and services to a discrete set of customers[2]) between entities.

A small business might exchange its services for money from a customer. A wholesaler might discount its products to gain access to a market provided by a retailer. Digital business—with its penchant for high-speed, low-cost communication between organizations—reduces the cost of value exchange, allowing for more complex business models. Over time, value networks become increasingly complex, while the stakeholders within these value networks become increasingly optimized.

The unfolding of the web ecosystem has borne this out. APIs have been a frequent channel for value exchange by powering business-to-business (B2B) process integration, underpinning app-based commerce, monetizing data, and more. This book will teach you how to use value dynamics to identify opportunities for growth and innovation in your digital business. *Value dynamics* is a visual method of designing business models through value networks and API-enabled value exchange. It will help you "place bets" on opportunities that arise from optionality.

Optimize Value Through Feedback Loops

The rapid communication that unlocks more complex value networks also allows organizations to gain a continuous understanding of their business. When an organization is exercising many options simultaneously, feedback loops are critical for knowing as quickly as possible which options are succeeding and which need to be shut down.

When organizations first create APIs, they often look at them as a means of providing data to consumers. However, APIs capture data as well. Leading digital businesses use APIs to collect feedback on business activities that can guide digital strategy. This book will show you how to cultivate effective feedback loops that can help determine when to double down on option bets and when to fold.

In combination, these techniques require a change in mindset that may be uncomfortable for many organizations. Rather than defining a detailed, long-term plan, successful digital organizations are much more focused on creating conditions for opportunities to flourish and capitalizing when they do. They recognize that each successful innovation will lead to unanticipated opportunities, so they aim to deliberately harvest unintended positive outcomes—happy accidents. This book teaches you to remember your "OOOps"—the winning methods of *optionality*, *opportunism*, and *optimization*—if you want to benefit from happy accidents.

Successful Treasure-Hunting Strategies

By analyzing digital success stories through the lens of the three winning OOOps techniques, this book introduces four winning strategies that any business can employ to thrive in digital business using APIs.

TABLE 0.1: Four Winning Strategies in the Digital Economy

Exchange Optimization	Adapt analog business models for the digital world, thus increasing the speed and scale of value exchanges while lowering coordination costs.
Distributed Innovation	Put innovative technologies in the hands of business users and high option products in the hands of customers to run rapid, well-measured experiments that pay off.
Capability Capitalization	Unbundle and rebundle business capabilities to create new products, services, and even highly profitable operating units.
Value Aggregation	Connect disparate value networks to create an integrated business model whose whole is greater than the sum of its parts.

This book will help you use each of these strategies in any industry to great effect. We will also show you how to combine the winning methods to discover your own strategies. The sky's the limit!

We've Seen This Approach Work

Throughout our professional careers, we have both helped organizations bring their business and technology teams closer together in the pursuit of digital success. In the course of our work with enterprises, we've seen the same patterns and antipatterns emerge. From the private to public sector and across every industry, we have found that the recipe for success in the digital economy comes from the unbundling approach we share here.

Through our collective work, we have extracted and articulated the practices companies employ to build successful digital businesses. We codified these strategies and methods and then helped other organizations—especially digital settlers—apply them and yield positive results. These engagements inspired us to write this book.

In our research, we interviewed more than twenty individuals from a variety of innovative companies and across a wide spectrum of roles: CEOs, CIOs, architects, consultants, and more. You will hear firsthand from these change agents. Although they differ in roles, you will see how they share a common worldview:

- They see APIs as mission-critical business assets, not as technical components.
- They have an "outside-in" view of their business, orienting on their value proposition for customers more than the operational competencies their enterprises are known for.
- They weigh their near-term opportunities against a high-level mission rather than trying to adhere to a rigid, long-term plan.

The elements of this shared mindset show up in the strategies and methods of unbundling.

You Have a Part to Play

If you are a business or technology professional involved in your company's digital transformation, this book can help you. The approach we prescribe will especially help you align your organization's transformation efforts with meaningful business objectives. The strategies and methods articulated here will bridge the gap between the digital intentions of the C-suite and the day-to-day work happening on the ground.

This book gives you a stake in your organization's transformation, whether you identify as a business leader or a technology professional. This is a book about connection: Connecting business to technology. Connecting long-term strategy to short-term return on investment. Connecting intuition to science. Anyone interested in helping their enterprise stay relevant in turbulent times will find value in this book.

Seeing It Through

To ultimately realize success, you will also need to confront some practical considerations. What are the organizational implications of taking this digitally native approach to business? What new risks are introduced in such a setup and how can they be mitigated? How can the approach be aligned with financial realities? This book answers all those questions.

For too long, business leaders have been trying to find their way in the digital economy through gut feel or by copycatting the surface characteristics of successful companies. This book goes beneath the surface, deconstructing those success stories into their essential lessons. This book shows that although the specific events or innovations may not have been intended, they occurred in environments that had been deliberately populated by API-enabled options. *Unbundling the Enterprise* defines a methodology for engineering those positive, unintended occurrences: a science of happy accidents.

Let's begin.

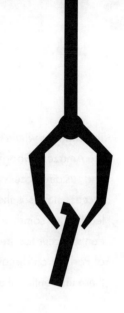

INNOVATION
BY
ACCIDENT

The chapters within Part I of this book explore the methods digital pirates like Amazon, Google, and Facebook used to fuel their explosive growth and sustain success over the last few decades. A curious pattern in these success stories is the prevalence of unintended events and innovations leading to some of their most positive outcomes. These "happy accidents" occur too frequently to be dismissed as coincidences. The focus of Part I is on discovering a methodology for intentionally engineering these unintentional outcomes, i.e., defining a science of happy accidents.

We will look at the common patterns adopted by digital pirates. To start, we will examine how these organizations have used APIs as foundational enablers for finding digital treasure. Through that examination, we will focus on three methods that lead to beneficial business conditions:

- Unbundling the digital landscape into API-enabled software components that provide discrete business capabilities, yielding a high degree of **optionality** within an organization's business environment.
- Rethinking business models through the dynamics of value exchange, thus providing a higher probability set of new business **opportunities**.
- Establishing feedback loops and reducing cycle time as a means of **optimizing** the digital operating model.

Each of these methods is explored in detail. Furthermore, we will show how digital pirates are not the only ones benefiting from these methods and the resulting happy accidents. We will also share stories of digital settlers who are finding success. It is time to set sail on the digital seas...

1

Treasure in Transformation

In 1882, Thomas Edison opened the first electrical power station in New York City.[1] To demonstrate the possibilities of continuous electrical power, Edison grabbed headlines by lighting up Lower Manhattan with electric bulbs. To everyone present, it was clear that the future had arrived.

But how could giant corporations that had emerged during the Industrial Revolution take advantage of this new power source? Their primary power source was steam, and they had spent the previous decades orienting their factories around steam boilers, optimizing the efficiency of steam power through new innovations, and creating a whole economy around steam-based products and occupations. Moving to a new power source would involve a lot more than unplugging steam and plugging in electricity. By 1900, only 5% of mechanical power was being provided by electricity.[2]

The tipping point for electrical power came from a new, electrically native industry. In 1913—thirty-one years after Edison's first power station—Ford Motor Company introduced the first moving assembly line for mass automobile production. This approach required discrete sources of power at multiple points along the process, something not possible with steam. By introducing a revolutionary manufacturing innovation that fueled the high-growth, job-producing automobile industry, Ford's assembly line helped unleash the electrical age.

Without being encumbered by antiquated approaches, the nascent automotive industry established many of the best practices for business in the twentieth century. Interchangeable parts, the division of labor, new management methodologies, and wholly controlled supply chains all became part of a business paradigm that spanned all manufacturing sectors. The model worked for the era. But those same practices that worked in the twentieth century don't seem to be as effective in the twenty-first century.

Today's period of digital transformation mirrors the shift from the steam age to the electrical age. It has been just over thirty years since the World Wide Web went online, the same amount of time it took for industry to transition from steam to electrical power. Companies formed within the last thirty years—Google, Amazon, Facebook—have grown to become some of the biggest in the world. These digital pirates have created new strategies and practices that fit the new age of business.

At the same time, many pre-web companies have struggled to optimize for digital business. Like early twentieth-century companies that adopted practices of the automotive industry, these digital settlers can learn from the digital pirates.

In this chapter, we will examine some of the common tools and practices digital pirates have used to thrive in the digital age. APIs are a factor, but it is how these companies use APIs that have led them to treasure. We will start with a source as surprising as a rolled-up piece of paper hidden in a pirate's boot.

The Yegge Platform Rant

One of the most detailed accounts of the digital pirates' inner workings was never intended to go public. In late 2011, Facebook was experiencing a meteoric rise and stood as the biggest threat to Google's dominance in web advertising revenue. Google's response was to launch the Google Plus social network. Google engineer Steve Yegge, who had previously worked at Amazon, posted a comparison of both Amazon and Google to the new social network. He thought it was being posted to a Google-only group, but it went out to the public at large. According to Yegge's own account, he drank some wine, published the post, went to bed, and awoke to find he was on the front page of the *Wall Street Journal*. The post had gone viral due to its sardonic candor. But what makes it continually relevant is its articulation of Amazon's platform approach.[3]

Yegge, whose background included a great deal of work building tools for developers, dedicates much of his rant to the distinction between the platform approach he experienced when working at Amazon and the non-platform approach he was experiencing at Google. He was especially frustrated that Google Plus lacked what he saw as key platform capabilities.

In Yegge's view, a platform is a software-based system whose functionality is broken into discrete capabilities that are made accessible to developers through APIs. Whereas a product strategy is about trying to anticipate market and user needs and then delivering packaged products to meet those needs, a platform strategy is about giving the right tools to developers to test their own ideas and build their own products and services. "Platforms are all about long-term thinking," he remarks.[4]

In other words, by giving this collection of building blocks to developers, providing the right incentives, and aligning the right business model, platform owners can significantly diversify their strategic options over the long term. Yegge saw this as a key to beat rival Facebook's success at that time. "Facebook is successful because they built an entire constellation of products by allowing other people to do the work," he notes.[5] (This approach of "distributing innovation" across its digital ecosystem is examined more in Chapter 7.)

Yegge lived through Amazon's transition from a product company to a platform company. Through that process, he observed how a company the size of Amazon was able to make it work. "The Golden Rule of Platforms is that you 'Eat Your Own Dogfood,'" he notes. "'Eat Your Own Dogfood' can be rephrased as 'Start with a Platform, and Then Use it for Everything.'"[6]

Yegge credits Jeff Bezos directly for establishing the platform culture at Amazon. "Bezos realized long before the vast majority of Amazonians that Amazon needs to be a platform," Yegge claims. "[He] realized that he didn't need to be a Steve Jobs in order to provide everyone with the right products...

He just needed to enable third-party developers to do it, and it would happen automatically."[7] It was a strategy that distributed innovation among third-party entities.

Around 2002, Bezos sent a memo to all Amazon employees, according to Yegge's account. The memo—now often referred to as the "Bezos API mandate"—was directed at Amazon's software development teams. It stated that all data and functionality must always and only be exposed via network-based interfaces (such as APIs) designed to be used by developers in the world outside Amazon, and these APIs must be the only interaction point between teams internally. Given that the "Dread Pirate Bezos," as Yegge refers to him, generally followed up his company edicts with ruthless governance, the organization took note and the platform culture took hold.[8]

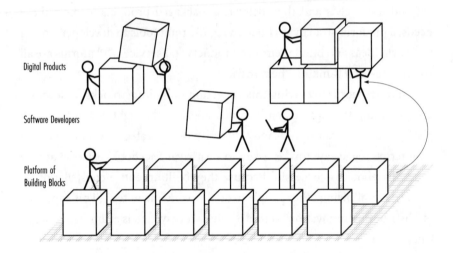

FIGURE 1.1: A Simplified View of the "Platform Approach" as Described by Steve Yegge

As Yegge recalls, "From the time Bezos issued his edict through the time I left, Amazon had transformed culturally into a company that thinks about everything in a services-first fashion."[9]

Amazon's platform culture led to a stunning run of product innovation. The API-enabled building blocks resulting from the platformization of Amazon.com were used to create offerings in new business domains, like third-party marketplaces, payments, and authentication, and as the foundation for the Kindle. The most conspicuous innovation enabled by the Amazon platform approach was the launch of Amazon Web Services, which now accounts for a significant chunk of the company's revenue and profits. This was the most obvious example of enabling third-party developers to build on the Amazon platform. It is likely no coincidence that at the same time Amazon adopted its platform culture, the company also expanded its focus beyond the original vision of being the "everything store" and being much more open-minded and opportunistic about entering any adjacent market it could move to quickly:[10]

1. All teams will henceforth expose their data and functionality through service interfaces.
2. Teams must communicate with each other through these interfaces.
3. There will be no other form of interprocess communication allowed: no direct linking, no direct reads of another teams' data store, no shared-memory model, no back-doors whatsoever. The only communication allowed is via service interface calls over the network.
4. It doesn't matter what technology is used: HTTP, Corba, Pubsub, custom protocols.
5. All service interfaces, without exception, must be designed from the ground up to be externalizable. That is to say, the team must plan and design to be able to expose the interface to developers in the outside world. No exceptions.
6. Anyone who doesn't do this will be fired. Thank you; have a nice day!

Yegge is one subjective source for this comparison of Google versus Facebook and Amazon, but the objective evidence supports his claims. The lesson here is that the platform approach adopted by Facebook and Amazon, and characterized using APIs, worked. The more closed, API-less approach Google used at the launch of Google Plus didn't.

Google would succeed with other products, which will be covered shortly. But first, let's look at Tim O'Reilly, one of the people who influenced Bezos's embrace of APIs.

Tim O'Reilly: The API Advocate

As early as 2000, Tim O'Reilly was enthusiastic about the possibility of the web as not just a collection of websites but as a platform of programmable capabilities that could be composed into novel services and embedded into new user experiences and devices. "Don't think of the web as a client-server system that simply delivers web pages to web servers," he remarked in his JavaOne Conference keynote in June 2000. "Think of it as a distributed services architecture, with the URL as a first generation 'API' for calling those services."[11] He specifically cited Amazon, eBay, E*Trade, and AOL as companies with data and functionality that could be unbundled and API-enabled to create this vast web platform.

Over the next two years, O'Reilly went on a personal mission to sell these companies and other web pioneers on his web-as-a-programmable-platform vision. AOL was unmoved by O'Reilly's pleas for it to open its recent MapQuest acquisition via APIs. Google responded conservatively by releasing their search function as an open API. According to O'Reilly, the most receptive company was Amazon. He was successful in getting an audience directly with the CEO. O'Reilly got Bezos's attention with an outside-the-box statement: "Amazon isn't just an e-commerce-site. It's become the information hub of the publishing industry."[12] Still, Bezos challenged O'Reilly to show how APIs could benefit Amazon. (Remember, this was two years before Bezos's API mandate.)

O'Reilly listed four reasons Amazon needed to adopt a platform culture by unbundling their capabilities through APIs. First, he used Microsoft as an example company that had repeatedly boxed out upstart competitors through their platform strategy. "Once you have other companies building added value that relies on you, you have a kind of benign industry lock in that's a real competitive advantage."[13] Here he predicted that MapQuest was likely to be marginalized by Microsoft's MapPoint service for this "product versus platform" reason. Second, O'Reilly noted that APIs would provide a gateway for all the smart and creative people who work outside of Amazon to create unanticipated innovation for the company. As O'Reilly put it, "Giving developers a playground extends your development staff, bringing in new ideas and features at the same time as it builds your brand and image."[14] The third area of value that O'Reilly articulated to Bezos was the claim that opening APIs would lead to new revenue opportunities for Amazon if they were willing to be patient. "Disruptive innovations often don't work all that well at first," O'Reilly pointed out. "So, you have to give them room to grow before you try to harvest them."[15] He cited Google's ability to offer free service at low volume and paid services at scale as proof. O'Reilly's final argument to Bezos was that the web functioned like an ecosystem: "The more life there is, the more there is for everyone."[16]

Bezos was clearly moved by O'Reilly's appeal. He followed up with O'Reilly shortly after the meeting to let him know that Amazon already had some web-based APIs in development. Bezos even brought some of his key Amazon leaders along when he attended O'Reilly's Emerging Technology Conference in April 2002, a conference that focused overwhelmingly on the possibilities of the web-as-a-programmable-platform. It lines up that Bezos issued his API mandate shortly after these encounters with O'Reilly.

There were internal forces driving API adoption at Amazon as well. In a 2020 interview with Harvard Business School, Andy Jassy—successor to Jeff Bezos as Amazon CEO—recounted how Amazon was able to unleash parallel innovation within the company. Amazon had initially instituted a "New Process Initiative" to prioritize funding for new ideas. However, this process became a bottleneck and a hindrance to innovation. In Jassy's words, "We'd have twenty good ideas and only be able to fund two."[17] They were able to unstick the process by addressing their software architecture. "Our software was too coupled," remembers Jassy. "It was really hard to manage."[18] Amazon's teams began unbundling their business capabilities into "well-documented, hardened Application Programming Interfaces"[19] to remove the coordination costs that were slowing down their projects. "That took us several years to address [....] getting all the teams to have these hard, well-documented APIs," says Jassy. "But that allowed us to, to kill the NPI (New Product Introduction) process so we could move it at a much faster rate."[20]

The constraints Amazon put in place to establish its platform culture had even more positive impacts than what O'Reilly had laid out. By forcing Amazon's own teams to communicate only through APIs, Amazon created a platform for external developers to innovate, setting the stage for developer-driven happy accidents to take place inside Amazon's walls. The mandate ensured that all of Amazon's software-based capabilities could easily be used internally to drive productivity and innovation, and only Amazon would decide which ones went public. That left room to keep select capabilities private to guard competitive advantage. Last, making every software service available to Amazon's developers lifted all of Amazon's boats, regardless of whether the tide rose for anyone else. Amazon had taken the platform approach to unforeseen heights.

Finding the Value of Google Maps

Picking back up on O'Reilly's vision for the future, it turned out that his warnings about MapQuest's lack of openness proved prophetic. However, it wasn't Microsoft's MapPoint that toppled MapQuest from its dominant position. Following Yegge's lamentation about Google Plus's lack of platform capabilities, he did tip his hat to a few Google products that were being designed and built with a platform mentality, even if it was against the current of Google's culture. One of those, Google Maps, provides even more insight into how packaged products can be unbundled into discrete capabilities that enable unanticipated innovations.

Launching as a product in early 2005, Google Maps aimed to dominate the online mapping market through its dynamic user experience, which contrasted favorably with market leader MapQuest's rigid UI. To enable the dynamic user experience, Google employed a new web architecture nicknamed AJAX (Asynchronous JavaScript and XML) that allowed client applications to send and retrieve data over the web without interrupting the user. This architecture required Google to host a Maps API on the server side that facilitated the preloading of data on the client side, allowing users to easily pan and zoom on their maps. Google Maps was lauded as a revolutionary web application, and its market presence began to grow.

Along the way, some savvy developers who didn't work at Google figured out how Maps was built and thought of new ways to use the technology. Rather than connecting to Maps through the UI, they sought to use the raw data from the server side to create visualizations in their own applications. To do this, they connected directly to the API that underpinned the Google Maps application. Sites like HousingMaps.com and ChicagoCrime.org were early adopters of this approach.

When Google recognized what was happening, they faced a dilemma. Technically, these developers were breaking the Google Maps terms and conditions. However, by integrating Google's mapping data with other information on the web, they were completely aligned with Google's mission "to organize the world's information and make it universally accessible and useful."[21] Ultimately, Google embraced what the developers were doing. In June of 2005, then Google Maps Product Manager Bret Taylor announced the launch of the Google Maps API as its own product in a brief blog post titled "The world is your JavaScript-enabled oyster."[22]

Although they shared a common data backbone, the Maps web app and Maps web API were different products, and they evolved differently. By allowing sites to embed mapping data—thus bringing Google Maps to the users instead of making them come to Google—the Maps API was instrumental in Google's initial goal of unseating MapQuest. However, up to that point, the product had been effectively "going with the flow." According to former Google Maps API Product Manager Thor Mitchell, "At first, the long-term value of the Maps API to Google, or how it could generate revenue, was not questioned....It was more like 'this seems like this is in line with our goals, so let's support it.'"[23]

In June 2006, a year after the initial launch, Google introduced a paid version of the Maps API, but that was less about establishing a new revenue stream and more about appeasing corporate clients who would not trust a free service. The blog post announcing the new Google Maps for Enterprise even states the new offering was created in "response to this popular corporate demand."[24] The potential value of the Google Maps API was apparent.

The mobile app boom that followed the launch of Apple's App Store in 2008 provided more opportunities to drive value through the Google Maps API. Its organic growth had been so steady that by 2011 the number of maps served by the Maps API exceeded the number served by the Maps web application.[25]

This got the attention of Google executives, and they worked with Mitchell and the team to solidify the Maps business model. First, as per its terms of service, Maps API usage could only be free for apps and sites that were free to users and universally accessible, in keeping with Google's mission. Second, limits were imposed to ensure the service was not being abused by consumers. This helped with cost recovery and avoidance, since half of the Maps API traffic came from a small set of highly trafficked websites, but it also led to some pushback from the customer community. Third, Google recognized that geolocation data would be central to its overall mobile strategy and worked to combine Maps and Places (check-in app) data to provide new personalized mobile experiences, as well as providing more precision in their targeted advertising business. By 2012, when Mitchell left his position as Maps API product manager, the number of apps and sites using the product had grown to more than one million.[26]

Google proceeded with the Maps product because it aligned with their corporate mission. The company observed within a few months of launching that customers wanted direct access to its Maps API, and Google was able to launch an API product only a couple months after that. In line with Tim O'Reilly's guidance to Jeff Bezos, the Google Maps team was "following its nose" as opposed to aiming for a fully realized product strategy. The Maps API kept Google's options open, allowing the company to act decisively as new opportunities arose. As a result, they gained first mover advantage. Later, they were able to react quickly to market dynamics—especially the mobile boom—to exploit the value of their Maps API product. "You make your own luck," as the expression goes. Serendipity in this case was only possible because Google had created the API option ahead of time.

H-API Accidents?

APIs played a big role in the growth and success of both Amazon and Google Maps. Amazon benefited from a top-down mandate that led to all its business capabilities being composable in new business lines and even business models. Google Maps took a more organic approach, following the wishes of its developer community to open via API and then riding the mobile boom to mass adoption. Neither company drew up a prescriptive five-year plan. So, are APIs the answer to success in the digital economy?

The good news is there are now many transformation success stories from companies that are digital settlers. Unsurprisingly, many of these have APIs as a common factor. Cox Automotive uses APIs to power its industry-leading marketplaces, such as Autotrader and Kelley Blue Book. Coca-Cola uses APIs to introduce new technologies across all its business lines and to crowdsource its product innovations. Capital One's APIs dynamically connect its customer channels with its core banking capabilities. Best Buy uses APIs to synthesize disparate lines of business. We explore each of these stories in later chapters.

As presented in the introduction, digital pirates have used APIs to find various forms of treasure: a viable business model for Facebook, a high-growth revenue stream for Google, the fulfillment of a grand vision for Amazon. However, this success did not just stem from the use of APIs. As we will see in the next chapter, these companies used three consistent methods to achieve these results. Those methods add up to an approach for uncovering happy accidents with APIs as the shovel.

2

The Science of
Happy Accidents

Legend has it that pharmacist John Pemberton created the secret formula for Coca-Cola by accident.[1] The story goes that while working on an alcohol-based painkiller using coca leaves and kola nuts, he decided to remove the alcohol in response to the temperance movement that was gaining popularity at the time. As the tale tells, he accidentally mixed sugar syrup and carbonated water with some of the original ingredients, leading to what would become the most well-known soft drink in the world. Whether this story is true or not, there have been many substantiated happy accidents like it in every era of business.

In 1966, Richard M. Schulze opened a new electronics store in his hometown of St. Paul, Minnesota. He named it Sound of Music to capitalize on the previous year's most popular movie. After growing the business modestly for fifteen years, it would be another classic film—*The Wizard of Oz*—that would prove a better analogy for the company's fate. In 1981, a tornado tore the roof off the biggest Sound of Music location. To make as much revenue as possible from the store's surviving stock, Schulze promoted a huge "Tornado Sale" featuring "best buys" on all remaining merchandise. The sale was a massive success and set the stage for the company to change its name to Best Buy, as well as change its go-to-market strategy to focus on low prices and high volume.[2]

After selling Flickr to Yahoo! in 2005, founder Stewart Butterfield started a game company called Tiny Speck that had some modest success with the multiplayer online game *Glitch*. Although that game failed to reach Butterfield's expectations, he recognized that the collaboration capabilities offered by the game had singular potential. To capitalize on this opportunity, Butterfield morphed Tiny Speck into a new company, Slack, and took aim at an entirely new class of customers with its new stand-alone collaboration product.[3]

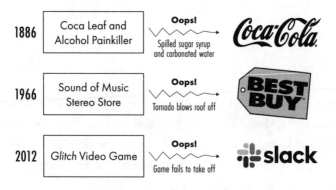

FIGURE 2.1: Happy Accidents Through the Years

In each of these situations (see Figure 2.1), an unsuccessful invention led to an unintended innovation. As the Slack example shows, the digital age has happy accidents too. However, as we have seen, the examples of Google Maps and Amazon Web Services seem to be less accidental than the legend of the Coca-Cola formula. Amazon and Google had strategies that enabled them to exploit new opportunities that arose from the combination of changing conditions in the marketplace and the capabilities they had created.

Combinatorial Innovation

There is a popular saying in the tech world that we overestimate the change that will happen in one year and underestimate the change that will happen in ten years.[4] This phenomenon is explainable. When people predict the future of technology, they often look at things linearly. For example, to predict the future of commuting to work, people might focus on the evolution of cars. This might lead them to exaggerate the projected adoption of self-driving cars. However, there are many interconnected conditions that could affect the future of how people get to work: alternative transportation mechanisms, the ratio of remote to in-person work, combined urban zoning, even the definition of work itself. It is likely that the concept of commuting will greatly evolve in the next decade, and that evolution will be affected by all the areas mentioned.

We underestimate longer-term change because we fail to see that innovation happens in combination. New innovations are built on a synthesized foundation of multidisciplinary capabilities. Consider one of the most impactful new technology paradigms of the twenty-first century: the mobile phone explosion circa 2008. The iPhone was not the first smartphone, but it was the innovation that introduced the new mobile paradigm. The iPhone itself contained some impressive hardware, but there were many conditions that led to its profound success that were external to the device.

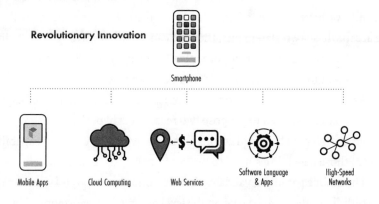

FIGURE 2.2: The Smartphone Innovation Was Enabled by Concurrent Capabilities

Here is a list of just some of the capabilities that allowed the mobile paradigm to take hold (see also Figure 2.2):

- Mobile apps and a mature World Wide Web provided engaging services that incentivized habitual usage of the new phones.

- Cloud computing provided highly available application infra-structure with elastic scalability and ubiquitous access.
- Web APIs provided a familiar way for app developers to connect to their own backend data as well as to fundamental third-party services such as telephony, payments, and geolocation.
- Mobile-friendly software languages and frameworks allowed highly motivated developers to ramp up quickly enough to launch their apps in good time.
- High-speed cellular networks provided the capability of piping the new volumes of mobile data.

A mobile phone expert from 1998 may have predicted touchscreen keyboards and high-resolution video playback, but it is unlikely they would have foreseen the App Store or the asymmetric treasure it delivered to Apple.

These examples illustrate a couple of points. First, the biggest innovations—the ones that offer the biggest business opportunities—tend to stem from a combination of innovations that happen in multiple related fields. Second, we have no way of knowing what those big innovations will be. If we accept these two statements, then we can see what's wrong with trying to build a five-year plan. Instead, organizations should focus on cultivating an environment in which happy accidents can take place.

As articulated above, innovation comes from a combination of capabilities. It makes sense then to propose two reasonable hypotheses when it comes to digital strategy: (1) organizations should strive to have a lot of capabilities, and (2) those capabilities need to be "combinable" or "composable."

The mobile paradigm validates these hypotheses on a grand scale. Amazon shows the hypotheses to be true on the level of a single organization. The Bezos mandate and its resulting institution at Amazon led to the creation of a tremendous number of capabilities. The mandate also ensured those capabilities were built in a composable way, as each capability could be accessed via API and therefore utilized within many processes and across many digital channels.

Both Google Maps and Slack show how specific capabilities can be made composable. Slack had a capability—multi-user collaboration and communication—built into its gaming context. This capability needed to be unbundled from the game to become composable. Once unbundled, the capability was turned into a product that served a much more generalized market.

From a technology perspective, Google Maps had an API for its UI-based product. However, it wasn't until third-party app developers reverse engineered the API that Google turned its API into a formal product. As described previously, that product became foundational to the mobile boom and provided new revenue and a new channel for Google's business.

These digital pirates didn't use a treasure map to find treasure. But they did use a consistent methodology, even if they didn't realize it at the time.

The Non-Rival Nature of Digital Products

Besides combinatorial innovation, there is another dynamic at play in the digital economy that accelerates the hurried pace of change. In a manufacturing economy, there are constraints that dictate the speed and cost of sourcing, storing, combining, and distributing physical goods. During the manufacturing boom of the twentieth century, companies like Ford would gain a competitive advantage by controlling their entire supply chain to minimize the impacts and unpredictability of those constraints. Digital products are different.

In economic terms, data is a *non-rival good*. A rival good is one that can only be consumed or possessed by one party at a time. Physical products are rivalrous. Two people cannot drive the same car to two different places at the same time. Non-rival goods, however, can be consumed or possessed by multiple parties simultaneously. People can stream the same songs and movies all at once. An original Bob Ross painting is a rival good, whereas a broadcasted Bob Ross television show is a non-rival good.

Rival products are limited by unit costs. The economic return on producing rival products is constrained by the cost of producing each item. Furthermore, their ultimate return is often capped by logistic constraints within their market. This leads to a *concave curve* when plotting their costs versus returns. Non-rival goods have the opposite property. Because each unit can reach an unlimited number of consumers, their potential returns are unconstrained by unit costs. This means they have a *convex curve* when plotting their potential returns versus production costs (see also Figure 2.3).

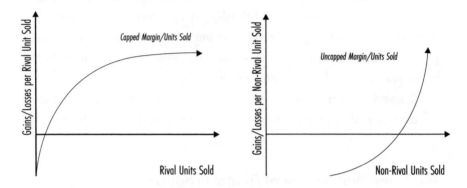

FIGURE 2.3: Concave vs. Convex Margin Curves of Rival and Non-Rival Products

Digital technologies make it easy to move data at speed and scale. They make it easy to store data cheaply. They make it easy to combine and transform data. However, it is also this economic property of data—its non-rival nature and subsequent replicability—that multiplies its economic potential. APIs are digital products whose material is data, making them non-rival products. Therefore, organizations launching successful API products create this potential for convex returns on their investment.

When it comes to returns on digital products, the degree of convexity is driven by the cost of experimentation. The cheaper it is for an organization to create, launch, and manage digital products, the steeper the curve on their returns. That's not to say that organizations should just launch as many digital products as possible. Instead, it's about how easily opportunities can be identified, how quickly the products can be assembled, and how readily their success or failure can be determined.

Digital pirates have used APIs to cheapen experiments. Having their business capabilities accessible via APIs accelerates the assembly of new products and services. Having these APIs reusable across channels and segments means they can easily be incorporated into new opportunities with minimal incremental cost. Digital pirates also use APIs to provide data on the performance of their experiments, which they use to increase returns by doubling down on successful ones and quickly shutting down failed ones. Thus, with APIs, experiments become cheaper, creating even more fertile ground for happy accidents. Taking all of this into consideration, let's now lay out a methodology for applying these principles in a practical way.

OOOps: A Science of Happy Accidents

Using the examples we've already walked through as well as several more we will study, we propose a science of happy accidents consisting of three methods. First, you need to create *optionality* by unbundling business capabilities through APIs. These API-enabled business capabilities are like your mechanical pirates digging for treasure.

Second, you need to use value dynamics to identify the *opportunities* that represent the best starting point for your experiments. We will explore value dynamics in detail in subsequent chapters, but for now, you can think about it as a way of finding the right island for your pirates to excavate.

Last, you need to establish the right feedback loops to help you *optimize* your innovation experiments. This helps your pirates know where to stop digging and where to double down. Collectively, we call these three methods—optionality, opportunity, optimization—*OOOps*. (See also Figure 2.4.)

- Create **optionality** through unbundled APIs.
- Identify **opportunities** through value dynamics.
- Drive **optimization** through feedback loops.

OPtionality   **OP**portunities   **OP**timization

FIGURE 2.4: OOOps: The Three Methods in the Science of Happy Accidents

Optionality Through Unbundling

As you approach your own life, do you make significant commitments as soon as possible or as late as possible? If you're seeking a new job, working with your children through the college application process, or even using an online dating app, do you commit to the first possible choice that comes your way or do you try to slow the decision down until more information becomes available? Slowing down the process of making commitments conserves optionality.

Using APIs to expose business capabilities allows an enterprise and its partners to slow down the process of making a commitment for exactly how a capability will be used, allowing the business to pursue multiple options at once. Software systems built using APIs allow optionality beyond the intended scope of an individual solution without significant sacrifice. In the case of Google Maps, Google never intended to turn its API into a paid product. However, because they chose not to lock themselves into a single context of use, businesses around the world were able to leverage the API to seek their own treasure. Rather than Google choosing to put a price tag on the API product, it was the users of the API who asked to pay for it to ensure that they could depend upon it as they incorporated Maps into their business models.

Optionality can be created in any software system. Consider a bank that wants to provide a self-service account open option for its retail customers. The bank would want this process to be as streamlined as possible, but at minimum, it would involve collecting customer information, checking credit scores, providing and vetting legal forms, giving choices for account types, and creating the new account, as well as tracking and communicating the status of the whole application. Figure 2.5 shows one way to solve it: build a monolithic web app that provides a self-service user interface and integrates with existing backend systems.

FIGURE 2.5: A Monolithic Web Application for Self-Service Account Open

This solution meets the stated requirements and that's it. But this same service could be delivered with a much higher degree of optionality. Figure 2.6 unbundles five capabilities from the web application and exposes them through APIs. The user experience remains the same, but now the bank has the option to take these capabilities out of the self-service account open context and use them in other ways. Customer information and retail account services can be leveraged at other customer service channels, such as in branches or at the call center. Document management and workflow tracking services can be used in numerous business processes. Credit scoring could conceivably be packaged and sold to third parties. Furthermore, the bank has more flexibility to make changes if this account open process needs to be augmented with new capabilities or if changes need to be made to its existing capabilities. The bank may not know what all the options are for the future, but it will be poised and ready through unbundling.

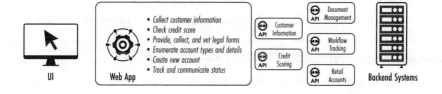

FIGURE 2.6: Self-Service Account Open Using Unbundled Capabilities via API

For decades, industry experts have advocated for modularity in software architecture, from early papers on information hiding through service-oriented architecture and microservices. However, choosing to make a decomposed architecture made up of discrete capabilities isn't just a technical choice. There are real financial benefits to creating decontextualized digital capabilities. Once unbundled in this way, these APIs can be rebundled into countless new contexts.

Opportunism Through Value Dynamics

Ultimately, the value of digital systems can be measured by how well they align with an organization's business model. Alexander Osterwalder, creator of the Business Model Canvas, defines business models as the way companies create, deliver, and capture value.[5] We expand on that to define *value dynamics* as a visual method for mapping out business models by illustrating the flow of value in a digital ecosystem. These business model maps use a few simple elements:

- Shapes to depict constituents in the ecosystem, such as companies or consumers.
- Arrows to show the flow of value between constituents.
- Icons that indicate what type of value "currency" is being exchanged. There are some obvious value currencies and some that aren't as intuitive.

Figure 2.7 shows a basic example of value dynamics using the relationship between a retailer's business model with that of a wholesaler in the same customer ecosystem. Obviously, the retailer purchases products from the wholesaler, which it then sells to end customers. However, visualizing the business model allows for the articulation of the retailer's unique role in the ecosystem. The retailer can buy products for a lower price from the wholesaler, since it is also providing reach to a targeted set of customers aligned with the wholesaler's products. On the other side of the picture, the retailer can mark prices up to consumers, since it is providing time savings and convenience in the form of store locations, product curation, customer service, and more.

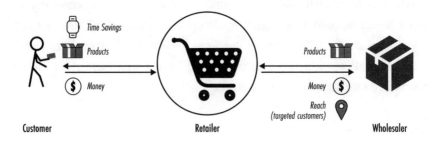

FIGURE 2.7: Simple Illustration of a Value Dynamics Map

Value dynamics allows you to illustrate a simple view of the value exchanges happening in your current digital ecosystem, thus depicting your business model according to the Osterwalder definition. Understanding how your business model works today, you can overlay what new capabilities or "options" you have; consider what value those capabilities capture, deliver, or create; and then see how that can flow between constituents in the ecosystem. From there, you can look for opportunities to add, augment, or eliminate value exchanges and even think through what new value can be captured on existing links. By using such a constrained set of items, the whole process can be gamified.

Optimization Through Feedback Loops

A common theme across the first two OOOps methods is lowering the cost of experimentation. Unbundling and optionality provide a faster and cheaper path to running experiments by providing digital building blocks. Value dynamics points the way to starting points that have a higher probability of yielding useful results. The third OOOps method—optimization—is about setting up feedback loops that help continuously decrease the cost of experiments and time to value.

Software movements such as Agile methodologies and DevOps stress the criticality of paving the path to learned insight. The notion of feedback loops and situational awareness are prevalent in any management methodology focused on dynamic environments. Back to the treasure hunt analogy, once those pirates start digging on the selected island, how do they determine when to stop digging or when to bring in more shovels? There are four main themes (see Figure 2.8) that emerge for how enterprises can ruthlessly lower the cost and time required for teams to create and test bundled and unbundled packages of value and deliver consumer-facing experimentation at scale.

Feature flags provide the ability to make targeted changes in API-enabled capabilities to controlled sets of audiences. From the color of a screen element to a change in the flow of screens for any user task to an alternate execution route via different APIs, feature flags can not only aid in optimizing the experiences of your developers and users but also help to control the risks and costs of your experiments.

Making it easy to segment traffic is the second tool to control the size of audience members receiving experimental changes. *Ramps* enable your experimentation teams to funnel a controllable percentage of all application traffic, again with simple configurations controlled via automation.

Just like a DevOps professional might use a waterfall chart to understand performance bottlenecks, your experiment teams will need robust *visualization* tools to make the efficacy of experiments self-revealing.

Finally, both *statistical literacy and tooling* are required to interpret the measurements derived from feedback loops. While the tooling capabilities are critical to making this approach work, it's equally critical to have a team of qualified humans to interpret the results. Both your business and technical teams need to be deeply familiar with the language and tools of statistics. Mature teams know that data beats math, and elite teams know that statistics tools can be misleading and cause speed-killing friction when you don't have the expertise to discern what the results mean and what they don't.

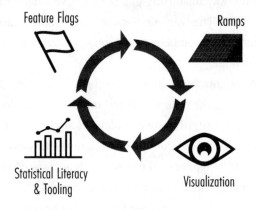

FIGURE 2.8: Four Feedback Mechanisms

In addition to these techniques, APIs create their own feedback loops. People commonly think of APIs as sources of data, a place where information can be retrieved or services can be requested. However, every API interaction creates contextual metadata that can be leveraged for other sources of value. Look at the example set by Google Maps. Maps consumers were happy to pay Google to get geolocation data in real time. But in so doing, those consumers were also providing information about their own locations and signaling intent by the requests they made. When the mobile boom happened, Google was able to profit from this geolocation context by using it in ad targeting, a strategy we will explore more deeply in Chapter 9. We will see many other examples where APIs have been used to drive useful strategic and operational feedback loops.

Feedback loops provide the instrumentation in your digital ecosystem. These four feedback mechanisms, and even APIs themselves, allow you to continuously measure value exchange and value impact in your ecosystem. Doing this will help you drive down the cost of creating new options and drive up the return on investment of exercising those options.

The three OOOps methods work most effectively together. If you just created APIs out of every software function in your environment, you might have a lot of options, but they could be rife with duplication and misaligned with the value-generating areas of your business. Value dynamics on its own could provide some useful starting points for digital innovation, but those opportunities would be difficult to explore without options and be merely speculative without feedback mechanisms. Last, feedback without a strategic direction would just provide a more accurate means of demonstrating stagnation. Combining the three OOOps methods, however, yields remarkable results.

OOOps for Digital Settlers

The OOOps methods haven't only been proven by digital pirates. Progressive Insurance is one digital settler who has utilized API-enabled unbundling to drive innovation. True to its name, Progressive has a history of disrupting the consumer insurance industry.

In the early 2000s, at the same time Amazon and Google were first introducing their web APIs, Progressive was already experimenting with APIs of its own. In its Claims group, Progressive launched an application called "total loss concierge" that helped drivers obtain financing if their vehicles had to be written off following a claim. To power the application, "[Progressive] used SOAP (Simple Object Access Protocol) to connect directly with banks to get financing options," recalls Geoff McCormack, one of Progressive's enterprise architects who remains with the company today.[6] This early move turned the company onto the value of unbundling through APIs, as well as the opportunism of digital ecosystems.

In the late 2000s, Progressive introduced Snapshot, a pluggable device that collected driving data used to assess drive safety. Customers could opt in to use this device to gain discounts on their auto insurance premiums. In the data-driven insurance industry, Progressive was able to disrupt the standard approach of pricing primarily on variables and instead utilize dynamic data. The company used an approach akin to the second OOOps method—opportunism through value dynamics—implicitly in this innovation. Furthermore, they were basing the innovation by optimizing through feedback loops (OOOps method #3) of driver information.

Progressive has also employed the first OOOps method: optionality through unbundling using APIs. For the last few years, Progressive has adopted an API-first approach to building its software systems that is paying dividends. Analyzing this unbundled landscape of business capabilities, Progressive recently launched a product targeted at small business customers that bundled its own APIs with a third-party, API-based insurtech provider of underwriting services. This brought the product to market in a matter of months, well ahead of expectations. "Our mindset is all around innovation, and we see the value in partnerships," McCormack states.[7] This ecosystem mentality is well-aligned with value dynamics.

Down to the Depths

Progressive Insurance is just one example of a company established prior to the web—a digital settler—figuring out the right approach to thriving in the digital economy. Although they weren't using a playbook for digital innovation, they adopted principles and practices used by the digital pirates to good effect. The next few chapters provide a playbook to leverage the learnings of digital success stories. We will go into each of the OOOps methods, illustrating how they work in action and how they combine to define a science of happy accidents.

3

Optionality Through API Unbundling

Thus far, we have discussed the accidental nature of innovation along with a high-level overview of the methods and strategies used by digital pirates to exploit the advantages of the digital landscape. We're now ready to dive deeper into the first OOOps method—optionality through APIs.

In this chapter, we aim to unpack exactly why APIs represent perhaps the best method available to organizations to create and preserve financial advantage relative to their competition. After completing this chapter, you will understand why the optionality created by APIs at scale represents the pinnacle of strategies to create the "land of a thousand shovels." To aid you in your efforts, we'll start by giving you the conceptual and financial tools necessary to understand and exploit API-based optionality.

Controlling Context Is Everything

Before starting an effort to formalize an unbundling or API initiative in your organization, it is important to know three things: (1) what optionality is, (2) what good looks like, and (3) what obstacles you must overcome to get your business teams fully on board.

First, optionality is simply defined as having the right to engage in many different options with no obligation to pursue any of them. At first glance, optionality doesn't seem to offer any particular benefit. Upon closer inspection, however, generating and preserving API-based optionality is a fundamental strategy for enterprises to remain relevant, maximize growth in the digital economy, and ultimately outperform relative to their peers and competitors. In terms of "what good looks like," let's return to our earlier ride-sharing scenario from the Introduction. More specifically, let's look at the Google Maps product that has become one of the most successful API products available.

Google Maps API

When you think of Google Maps, the typical mapping and navigation experience used by drivers or travelers probably comes to mind. But this fully contextualized product is not the only way Google Maps can be used. As we stated in Chapter 1, there is another scenario that is more frequently used than the web and app versions combined—the Google Maps API product.

An API product is sometimes referred to as a "headless" or "decontextualized" product because it doesn't have a visual interface that a person can easily engage with. This lack of a visual interface makes it possible for the API product to be consumed by other software programs. These programs can then decide how to use the data and functionality provided by the API later. A product in this form is more akin to a raw ingredient meant to be incorporated into another product. Just like baking flour is meant to be combined with other ingredients (e.g., to make a cake) and not eaten by itself, an API product is meant to be combined with other ingredients before being used by humans. As shown in Figure 3.1, the Google Maps product supports a fully contextualized experience alongside an API-based version that forgoes any contextualization, leaving room for consumers of that API to do with it as they will.

By building the visual maps product on top of an API (the web and mobile app products for Google Maps use the Maps API to render the maps and routes), Google has created an option for itself—the option, but not the obligation, to allow third-party consumers (e.g., Lyft, Uber, Airbnb, Yelp!, etc.) to pay for high-volume access to the API, so that the third-party consumers can produce value for their users and customers.

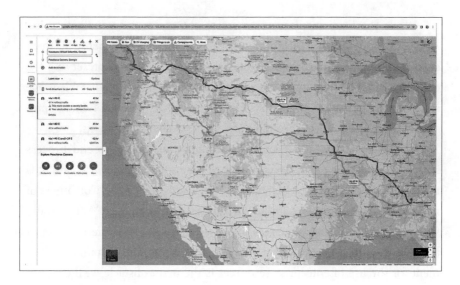

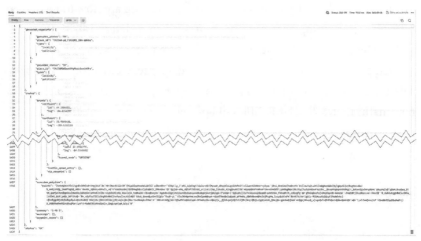

FIGURE 3.1: Illustration of Contextualized vs. Decontextualized Products

When looking at your enterprise's products and capabilities, including the various processes and business functions needed to bring them to market and offer them to consumers, has your enterprise constrained these capabilities to be used only in pre-ordained scenarios? Conversely, has your enterprise built its digital capabilities so that every discrete part can be made easily available to an interested consumer who has their own ideas about how to use those capabilities to create value for themselves?

While there are many ways to create optionality for your enterprise, APIs have a unique leverage point in reducing friction and expense between suppliers and consumers. When done at scale, creating and preserving the option to easily pivot your digital capabilities into other unpredictable usage scenarios defines "what good looks like," because API-based optionality preserves high-value choices through a series of low-cost investments.

While the technical aspect of breaking down an end-to-end process into small units of work is straightforward for a software delivery team, it is not always a simple task to get all stakeholders aligned on the worthiness of making the investments when the outcome is undefined (e.g., "Why should we invest our time and resources into use cases and consumers that can't be specifically described or identified?"). This difficulty in attaining alignment for the use of enterprise resources is the main obstacle we'll cover in this chapter. In short, finance and executive leadership are slow to recognize and support anything that can't be expressed in a deterministic financial model. The lack of a clear set of industry-vetted best practices has created a shared perspective across many of the leaders interviewed for this book—there is a need for a new lens on how to view business forecasts along with a "new math" that will drive a different approach to investment and continual transformation.

The Search for a "New Math"

Business and technology leaders are not alone in the search for a "new math." The quest for the quantitative insight necessary to pave the road for the "new math" has been underway for several decades. In her work as an economist, Dr. Carliss Y. Baldwin, author and Professor of Business Administration, Emerita at the Harvard Business School, has made significant progress in bringing much-needed clarity to the economic benefits of modularity and optionality.

Baldwin has taken the path of detailed economic analysis to present a ground-level truth on the quantitative value of modularity and optionality. To quantify and understand the financial value of modularity, Baldwin has produced multiple works, most notably *Design Rules: The Power of Modularity* and *The Architecture of Platforms: A Unified View*, as well as contributed to *Platforms, Markets, and Innovation*. Looking closely at Baldwin's work on technology-enabled platforms, we can begin to see the form of a "new math" emerge when she specifically explores the question: When should an enterprise leverage optionality to create and exploit a platform strategy?

> Option value is low when consumer tastes are homogeneous and predictable, and designs are on a tightly determined technological trajectory (Dosi, 1982). In such cases, it is usually obvious what will succeed in the market, hence the value of multiple experiments and diverse approaches is low. Option value is high when consumer tastes are heterogeneous or unpredictable, and technological trajectories are uncertain. In these cases, it is not obvious what will succeed, hence the value of multiple experiments and diverse approaches is high.[1]

Baldwin's perspective on higher option value being present "when consumer tastes are heterogeneous or unpredictable, and technological trajectories are uncertain" is specifically interesting because it is directly provable in the context of financial markets. To see the impact of technological unpredictability play out in a measurable financial context, we'll shift our focus from Baldwin's work to the perspective of a different, and often more provocative, leader: Nassim Nicholas Taleb.

Over the last twenty years, Taleb has written a five-volume work notably containing *The Black Swan* (referred to by the *Sunday Times* as one of the twelve most influential books since World War II[2]) and *Antifragile: Things That Gain from Disorder*. Taleb's career as an author, mathematical statistician, former option trader, and risk analyst has consistently revolved around problems of randomness, probability, and uncertainty. Within *Antifragile*, Taleb discusses and models the economic benefits that come from optionality. He helps clarify and quantify these benefits by introducing a structure to classify options into two different types: concave options and convex options.

These two types of optionality can be understood by looking at three factors:

1. The incremental cost (pain) to generate and maintain the option (the right to engage the option with no obligation to pursue it).
2. The potential value (gain) that could come when you exercise the option.
3. How the value scales when the rate of change (variable) scales on the y axis.

Just like the concave and convex curves for rival versus non-rival products discussed in Chapter 2, the same is true for understanding and forecasting the value of options. When the cost to generate and maintain the option is high but the potential gain from exercising it is low, that option is said to be concave (shown on the left in Figure 3.2). Conversely, when the cost to generate and maintain the option is low but the potential gain is high, that option is said to be convex (shown on the right in Figure 3.2).

When examining the graphs in Figure 3.2, it is critical to notice that the pain/gain measured in the y axis rockets up as X (where X is uncertainty or variables) increases. What Taleb is pointing out is that in systems where (a) the future is uncertain and inherently unpredictable and (b) optionality can be preserved at low cost, the potential gain to be had by creating and preserving optionality is staggering because "uncertainty increases the upside but not the downside."[3]

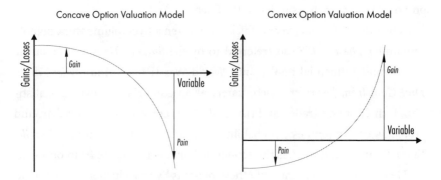

FIGURE 3.2: Concave vs. Convex Valuation Models for Options
Source: Nassim Nicholas Taleb. *Antifragile: Things That Gain from Disorder.*
New York: Random House, 2014: 273.

In contexts where uncertainty is high (what Dr. Baldwin describes as "when consumer tastes are heterogeneous or unpredictable, and technological trajectories are uncertain"[4]), both Dr. Baldwin and Taleb give the exact same advice—the best strategy is to have LOTS of bets where you can control the costs (i.e., a thousand shovels). Taleb then goes one step further and explains, "This allows us to minimize the probability of missing rather than maximize profits should one have a win, as the latter [maximize profits] strategy lowers the probability of a win. A large exposure to a single trial has lower expected return than a portfolio of small trials."[5]

When speaking or writing on convex optionality, Taleb is dogmatic about a basic principle relating to how technology develops within society. The attempts to use human understanding as a tool to predict future events are made in vain given that the prediction of future events in the modern world is impossible. Furthermore, when compared with an approach that embraces convex optionality, taking a "knowledge-based" approach is, in fact, foolish given the amount of money you're leaving on the table.

In the world of options trading, Taleb's guidance is to abandon your sense of knowledge and instead look for systems with asymmetry between pain (the cost to develop and maintain an option) and gain (the possibility of upside from possessing the option). When the pain is small and fixed compared to the potential gain (convex option), Taleb advocates for many small bets to maximize the likelihood of achieving a large gain.

One nuance to understand when considering Taleb's valuation models is how he models and leverages serial optionality, where winning options build upon each other to attain asymmetric gains. Amazon used serial optionality to find its way when it developed sustained demand for its first cloud offerings (a set of e-commerce APIs in 2004) and then launched a small set of software products (S3, SQS, and EC2) that are the foundation of AWS offerings and then doubled down yet again to continually reinvest and innovate more cloud-based offerings. Today, AWS captures more than $100 billion in revenue.[6]

In other words, in convex environments (where cost is low but potential gain is high), success can be found by systematically capturing and building upon a small set of winners from a large set of small bets placed via trial and error.

Using trial and error in a convex environment (referred to by Taleb as convex tinkering) can yield large benefits compared to the application of "applied knowledge" or "random chance." To illustrate this, Taleb uses a random simulation with three approaches (shown in Figure 3.3).[7]

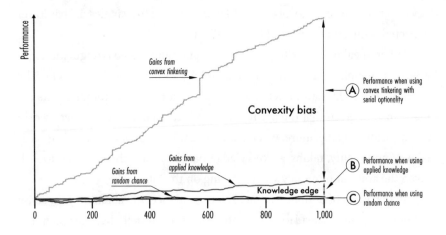

FIGURE 3.3: The Antifragility Edge (Convexity Bias)
Adapted from Nassim Nicholas Taleb. "Understanding Is a Poor Substitute for Convexity (Antifragility)." Edge. December 12, 2012. https://www.edge.org/conversation/nassim_nicholas_taleb-understanding-is-a-poor-substitute-for-convexity-antifragility.

The simulation models and executes three strategies to show "the difference between (a) the process with convex trial and error (antifragile), (b) a process of pure knowledge devoid of convex tinkering (knowledge based), (c) the process of nonconvex trial and error, where errors are equal in harm and gains (pure chance). As we can see, there are domains in which rational and convex tinkering dwarfs the effect of pure knowledge."[8]

Through an approach of lots of small bets where you can control the costs, you can, through convex tinkering, maximize your chances of finding the "Big Discovery" in the form of a "Positive Black Swan" (shown in Figure 3.4) because, "Any trial and error can be seen as the expression of an option, so long as one is capable of identifying a favorable result and exploiting it, as we see next."[9]

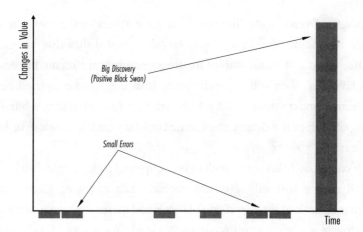

FIGURE 3.4: Manufacturing Positive Black Swans
Adapted from Nassim Nicholas Taleb. *Antifragile: Things That Gain from Disorder.*
New York: Random House, 2014: 182.

Greybeard and Bob Go Ashore

For readers who are not deeply versed in the financial models of Wall Street traders, let's see if our two pirates from the prologue can lend a hand. To keep the two models straight in your head, you can visualize the curves as frowny and happy faces (shown in Figure 3.5). Concave is bad (because the upside is limited, and costs are not) and convex is good (because the upside is unlimited, and costs are controlled).

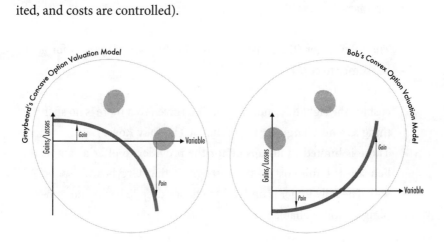

FIGURE 3.5: Convex vs. Concave Models for Options
Source: Adapted from Nassim Nicholas Taleb. *Antifragile: Things That Gain from Disorder.* New York: Random House, 2014: 273.

Imagine Dread Pirate Greybeard has gone ashore in the port where his favorite restaurant, The Jolly Roger, serves several dishes that he and his crew like to eat. When the staff of the Roger hands him a menu, he sees two of his favorites along with a newly added dish that he's never tried before. Greybeard wonders if he could ask the wait staff to bring him a bite-sized serving of each of the three dishes so he could try each one before ordering a full serving.

Of course not! He's got to stick to the script and pick a single dish because The Jolly Roger isn't willing or able to make tasting plates, given that the kitchen is optimized for a set menu of meals and there's nothing in it for them except lower operating margins. Similarly, Greybeard is also unlikely to order and pay for all three dishes just to make sure that he gets the one he likes best. From the perspective of the owner of The Jolly Roger, what's the likelihood that a customer will buy more than one dish because they allowed you to taste them before ordering? Answer: not likely.

The value of offering these bite-sized samples (options) is concave (high pain and low gain) for the restaurant because the cost to create samples of the dishes is relatively high and the benefit is low, given that a sample is unlikely to make the customer buy more than one dish. The gain associated with this option could be reasonably valued at or near zero.

In summary:

- The Jolly Roger (the provider) has a healthy set of options for a consumer to consider.
- Greybeard (the consumer) must take on a relatively large, fixed cost for the right to sample any option (given that there is no such thing as a no-charge "tasting plate" at The Jolly Roger).
- There is limited to no upside for the provider to offer a sample beneath the full cost of the dish given that Greybeard's spend with The Jolly Roger is unlikely to change despite having no sampling option available.

Conversely, Captain Bob heads to his favorite brewpub, The Mermaid's Call. Like many pubs, The Mermaid's Call offers free samples of a few of their many beers. Here the economics of offering samples are reversed because of three factors:

1. The "sample servings" give the provider the capability to keep the cost of a customer sampling of one or more options very low when compared to the total order size from the customer.
2. The likelihood that a customer will spend money for more servings (based on the sample) is high.
3. The upside for the provider (i.e., the potential value of the customer order) is both variable and disproportionately large when compared to the cost of providing one or more samples (e.g., maybe it will inspire Captain Bob to bring an entire keg back to the ship for his thirsty crew).

Rules for Preserving and Exploiting Convex Optionality

Accepting the precept that luck beats knowledge doesn't suggest organizations should wait around and hope that luck will deliver the next big breakthrough and change the world. Instead, the lesson Taleb is trying to communicate is that if you understand the futility of trying to predict the future in an uncertain world, then manufacturing and preserving convex optionality (i.e., being prepared to deliver bite-sized chunks of value in many different combinations at a low cost) is the surest way to outperform the competition over time. The more uncertain the future, the greater the value of preserving optionality. In this frame, once you have the information necessary to make ground-truth conclusions, all you must do is make rational decisions to capture the gains from the changes as they happen.

Taleb articulates a set of seven rules for preserving and exploiting convex optionality. For the purposes of developing a new math to satisfy financial stewards, we've condensed this list to four rules that can easily be communicated:[10]

1. Convexity is easier to attain than knowledge. Convexity can be increased by lowering costs per unit of trial (to improve the downside).

2. A convexity strategy can be executed by (a) lowering costs per unit of trial and (b) increasing the number of trials as large as possible. This minimizes the probability of missing the winning option rather than maximizing the profits of a winning option.

3. Preserving serial optionality beats a strategic plan. Long-term strategic plans tend to have the side effect of restricting optionality by locking teams and systems into rigid models and policies, or as Taleb says, "like a highway without exits."[11]

4. Get into the habit of cataloging negative results. Optionality works by cataloging negative information along the lines of Edison's famous quote: "I have not failed. I've just found 10,000 ways that won't work."

Once the idea of convex tinkering is laid out, a new approach begins to emerge. This is evident in examples of modern enterprises that have embraced and oriented themselves around serial optionality.

A best practice that is part of the DNA of the Salesforce enterprise is to "let tactics dictate strategy." This principle is one of the most important ideas that allowed the Salesforce platform and its surrounding ecosystem to grow and thrive at an accelerated pace. All Salesforce teams and product leaders know the power of Lean experimentation to allow for a clearer view of actual opportunities rather than ones we might imagine without the data to support them.

The Bezos API mandate at Amazon (as we explored in Chapter 1) required all systems to communicate via APIs that could conceivably be used by parties external to Amazon with no room for exceptions. Per Steve Yegge, a former development engineer/manager at Amazon and then Google, "Bezos realized that he didn't need to be a Steve Jobs to provide everyone with the right products: interfaces and workflows that they liked and felt at ease with. He just needed to enable third-party developers to do it, and it would happen automatically."[12]

The Coca-Cola Company entrusts its employees to steward what is perhaps their most important asset—the Coca-Cola brand. When the teams at Coca-Cola were interested in finding an efficacious way to protect the brand within retail environments, convex optionality paid off big. In a previous project, the IT team had implemented an AI-based service that could interpret photos of shelves to rapidly produce inventory counts (rather than the tedious and error-prone methods of hand counting). Because the development team retained the optionality to utilize the AI service abstractly, the already-established capability was easily directed to the task of detecting deviations in the stocking of Coca-Cola-provided coolers at retail establishments. Rather than tasking logistics teams with the intrusive task of photographing coolers within a delivery process, Coca-Cola enlisted their customers to "show their love" for the brand by photographing the coolers where they were buying their beverages for a small discount on future purchases. This minimal investment in modularity gave Coca-Cola a tremendous upside. The new capability allowed Coca-Cola to control how its products were presented and merchandised in retail establishments, strengthened brand loyalty with consumers, and ultimately drove higher sales.[13]

Upon reading this chapter, we know it's possible that some will walk away and think we're advocating for enterprises to adopt a mindset centered around gambling. This couldn't be further from the truth. To understand the difference here, you only need to know one thing: Casinos don't gamble. Casinos provide entertainment to guests and work the math at scale.

To make this concept completely clear, you can ask yourself one basic question: If casinos were indeed gambling, how is it possible that they all stay in business and have fairly predictable returns?

There's no trick question or clever distinction to share here. Casinos don't have better luck on their side. It's as simple as it looks. Casinos do not gamble. Casinos act as "the house" and have a deeply institutionalized grasp of probability and statistics. Based on how distributions of winners and losers occur in any one game, casinos take one of two postures:

1. Casinos allow patrons to make bets against the house in scenarios where the probability odds *always* favor the house by a measurable margin. Whether it's blackjack, roulette, craps, or slots, the house has a measurable edge in all these games because of the game rules set by the house. At scale, it's just not possible for a casino to consis-

tently lose. Of course, it's possible for casinos to lose an individual bet or even, in rare cases, have a losing day overall. But the odds are just too stacked in the casino's favor for those cases not to be the slim exception.

2. Where casinos can't control the odds, they set the patrons against each other and take a neutral position while garnering a cut of bets (known as the rake), which ranges between 2.5% and 10% of the stakes in play.

When we're advocating to create and conserve convex optionality with many small bets, we're talking about adopting the position of the house and working the math at scale. Will all bets win? Of course not. It's not even that most bets will win. The distinction is the potential for asymmetric value returned when a bet wins. This happens when you play more variants while taking steps to lower the cost of playing each variant out to the end.

Manufacturing Convexity Through Optionality

Once an organization has aligned the financial value at stake with a strategy that embraces optionality, the next question to address starts from Taleb's four rules for preserving and exploiting convex optionality that we explored in the previous section (see pages 39 and 40). More specifically, the question to consider is: What tactics will be the most efficient and effective at lowering the costs per unit of a trial?

This is the most foundational question you need to answer in an unbundling initiative because your ability to find unknown treasure will be driven by how many trials your organization can run at once (i.e., How wide can Captain Bob spread his mechanical army of hole diggers?). Without a clear path to lower the cost of an experiment, most organizations will not be able to afford a wide enough range of experiments to find options with the potential for asymmetric returns. As proven by Amazon in the quote from Andy Jassy in Chapter 1, this is where APIs become the focal point of your strategy to find new ways to deliver value through an unbundled set of packaged business capabilities.

To help digital settlers make the journey from a tightly coupled operating model with rigid infrastructure and applications that make experimentation expensive and time-consuming (i.e., concave optionality) to a new world capable of handling a wide number of small experiments cheaply (i.e., convex optionality), let's look at three stages of maturity that organizations inhabit.

Stage 1: Highly Concave

As shown in Figure 3.6, the starting point for many organizations is one where leadership and delivery teams are deeply frustrated given an inability to make changes or launch experiments without accruing large costs and long lead times.

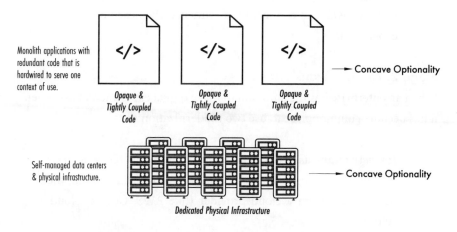

FIGURE 3.6: Concave Optionality Due to Operational Rigidity

Much of the frustration is driven by two factors that bottleneck the ability of an organization to conduct multiple experiments in parallel:

1. The dependency on the self-managed data centers and physical infrastructure.
2. The dependency on monolithic applications that are hardwired for a single context of use.

This setup is highly concave because an organization with this type of infrastructure:

- Is forced to incur large effort and cost when they want to make changes within the physical computing environments (e.g., creating a new test environment for a new experiment).
- Is forced to incur large effort and cost when they want to make changes within the monolith applications (e.g., decouple the data service that powers a business application for a new/different use case).
- Endures a low return on the effort and cost of experiments due to the small number of changes that the organization can push through the delivery system at one time (because an organization will not be able to run many experiments when each one is very expensive).

Stage 2: Partially Transformed

When an enterprise has the ambition to make digital experimentation easier, it has become commonplace to use two modernization tactics.

1. **Infrastructure as a Service (IaaS):** Commonly referred to as "migration to the cloud" or a "cloud transformation," using the data centers from a cloud provider (like AWS, Google Cloud, Azure, etc.).
2. **Multi-Variable Testing (MVT):** MVT tools are often composed of feature flags, traffic management via ramps, statistical tooling, and visualization.

The combination of these two tactics begins to loosen the constraint of how many experiments can be run in parallel without incurring exorbitant expenses. When these two tactics are applied, an enterprise enters the second stage of convexity: partially transformed.

As shown in Figure 3.7, many organizations have begun modernization initiatives that will utilize the IaaS and MVT tactics for consumer-facing experiences. These efforts yield positive results by reducing the friction and expense incurred for changes and experiments by:

- Decoupling software delivery from self-managed infrastructure (e.g., a sprint team can create or destroy a set of environments with a cloud provider with nominal lead time and expense).
- Enabling consumer experience teams to leverage feature flags, ramps, and statistical tooling (e.g., a delivery team can control the audiences exposed to an experiment, along with any business risk associated with the experiment, and can understand the results of the experiment with nominal lead time and expense).

In this partially transformed state, the constraints on changes and experiments are only partially loosened because teams must still incur the time and expense of working with highly complex code that is conceptually tied to a single context of use. The ability to create and conserve optionality varies and is specifically concave for scenarios that involve software-based consumption of core capabilities or that are beyond a singular context of use.

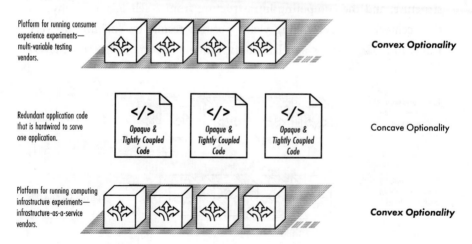

FIGURE 3.7: Partially Concave Optionality Due to Tightly Coupled Code

Concave optionality can be fully seen in the Google Maps example. Imagine Google had built its Maps offering with a set of internal-use-only services and a tightly coupled (non-API-based) method for communicating the mapping data from Google's infrastructure to a user's web browser or mobile app. What level of expense would Google have to incur to make it possible for a software-based consumer to access the same data and integrate that data into its own business applications? Would Uber, Lyft, and the other map-dependent companies have been as fast to emerge? It's arguable that they might not have emerged at all because they would have had to build all the mapping capabilities on their own, which would have changed the ROI for the venture firms that supported them.

By choosing to take a modular, API-based approach, Google dramatically reduced the cost of allowing third parties to use their data in novel ways and ultimately hit the jackpot by embracing serial optionality and becoming the name brand associated with API-based mapping services.

Stage 3: Highly Convex

As shown in Figure 3.8, a fully transformed organization has attained a high degree of convexity by decoupling each of the capability layers from each other (e.g., consumer experience from capability, the capabilities from infrastructure, and the computing infrastructure from a self-managed physical data center). This decoupling yields positive results by enabling delivery teams to make changes and launch experiments at any of the three layers where value is created.

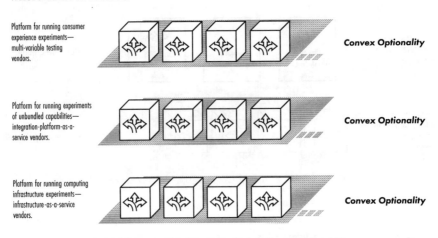

Platform for running consumer experience experiments—multi-variable testing vendors.

Convex Optionality

Platform for running experiments of unbundled capabilities—integration-platform-as-a-service vendors.

Convex Optionality

Platform for running computing infrastructure experiments—infrastructure-as-a-service vendors.

Convex Optionality

FIGURE 3.8: Increased Convex Optionality from Unbundled Capabilities

In this new operating state, changes and experiments are unconstrained because the capabilities that power experiences can be brought to market as singular offerings or in combination with any other capability without requiring large IT expenses or long delivery lead times. The ability to create and conserve optionality is optimized at each layer where value is created inclusive of scenarios that involve non-human consumption (e.g., a ride-sharing service utilizing a set of mapping or GPS APIs) or multiple contexts of use.

Transforming Options into High-Value Interfaces

To optimize the convexity of your API-based optionality, there are three major factors to consider and work with. The first is to recognize and align with the financial model for non-rival products (where profit margins skyrocket as an offering scales). The second involves provisioning the capability to launch many API-based digital experiments at low cost. The third tactic involves making specific packaging choices to maximize the possibility of achieving the uncapped, asymmetric return as predicted by Taleb.

Given that Taleb's valuation model is more commonly applied with financial options traded at an exchange, Taleb does not share any API-centric guidance on how experiments might be guided to achieve higher upsides (outside of leveraging serial optionality). To find the path to the highest ROI opportunities, we must return to Dr. Baldwin's work on modularity and platform economics.

Within *The Architecture of Platforms*, Baldwin concludes her analysis with a few crisp ideas that can help enterprises maintain long-term value from the options that they maintain via modularity and composability. First, controlling the interfaces to value rather than just the systems that deliver value is the better strategy. Baldwin exposes IBM's well-known blunder with PCs. Rather than maintaining control over the critical interfaces to value—

(1) the Basic Input/Output System (BIOS), which insulated software developers from the hardware so that new devices could be added without rewriting programs; (2) the instruction set of the Intel 8088 chip, the basic

commands into which all software had to be translated; and (3) the operating system, a set of 'higher level' services that human programmers could
use instead of accessing the BIOS or CPU directly[14]

—IBM made intentional decisions to focus on controlling how the value itself
was created.

Baldwin notes:

> All of these interfaces have survived to the present day....What was prob-
> lematic for IBM in the PC platform architecture was that IBM controlled
> only one of three critical interfaces, namely the BIOS. This interface, more-
> over, was simple and not tightly integrated with other parts of the system.[15]

This effectively left IBM on the sidelines for the PC revolution of the
1980s that made Microsoft and Intel into global juggernauts.

> This example teaches us that in a man-made platform, the interior of the
> core—the part hidden behind the interfaces—is not an essential part of
> the platform. In contrast, the interfaces are essential: the PC interfaces have
> lasted much longer than their hardware implementations, and their strate-
> gic significance has been profound.[16]

Baldwin also explains a foundational concept for how modularity and
platforms create value and optionality—open by default is a better strategy
than closed by default. Baldwin quotes another giant of modern software, Bill
Joy, a founder of Sun Microsystems, when he famously said, "Not all smart
people work for you." She then posits the corollary of this: "Smart people are
hard to find but may find you if you open up your platform."[17]

Among the most important decisions an organization can make is where
and when to package value and make it open to teams throughout an organization or even to the outside world. While fully open is not necessarily
always the right thing to do, it's clear that fully closed systems (i.e., monoliths)
are non-starters in today's interconnected and hyper-specialized world. The
concept that enterprises, and the teams within them, should align with is that

the incremental value they produce along a value chain can be immense, but you'll only be able to receive the full value being created if you preserve the option (via modularity) to make it open.

Returning to the casino analogy, choosing the right interface to a valuable digital service is akin to making yourself "the house," where most/all roads lead to you with asymmetric upsides, like AWS, Google Maps, and Slack.

When you choose a popular and easy-to-understand interface, it is critical to make sure that your chosen interface won't be too easy to commoditize (this is why Netflix created and then spun off Roku into a separate company—because they understood that streaming hardware, like the Amazon Fire TV Stick or Google Chromecast device, was going to quickly become a commodity with low margin potential) or too easy to abstract (as in the IBM PC core from Baldwin's earlier example). You can still generate a lot of revenue, but your returns are capped because you've ignored how non-rival margin curves work or you've made it too easy for a competitor to position themselves between you and your consumers.

Three fundamental behaviors emerge when you combine Baldwin's work on platform economics with Taleb's work on optionality:

1. Generate and preserve composability via controlled interfaces to small chunks of modular value.
2. Learn how and where to leverage your composable capabilities by understanding where, how, and why value is exchanged between parties in your ecosystem (covered in Chapter 4).
3. Preserve optionality by making it possible to offer those chunks of value to other parties at a low cost, which you then further preserve by continually lowering the cost of generating future options (covered in Chapter 5).

It is not a coincidence that these three behaviors are strikingly like the capabilities outlined in the OOOps methods. Whether referring to Baldwin's model of creating value through modularity or the experiences of any of the digital leaders interviewed for this book, the tactics to create and capture the value from API-based digital products remain the same.

The secret to the success of this approach lies in understanding how value is created with optionality. When organizations build software-based solutions out of components that can be further leveraged in the future, unknown scenarios—i.e., building systems with convex optionality—these companies set themselves up to jump on future opportunities quickly. Taleb elaborates on this concept, stating, "If you 'have optionality,' you don't have much need for what is commonly called intelligence, knowledge, insight, skills, and these complicated things that take place in our brain cells, for you don't have to be right that often."[18]

Embracing Modularity by Default

Whether you plan to capture a first-to-market advantage with a ground-breaking digital offering or choose to moderate your risk with a fast-follower posture, the time has come to adopt and formalize a set of architectural rules around the use of APIs as the mechanism to create fine-grained, reusable building blocks of value. Deferring the "small pain" of "modularity by default" will undoubtedly cripple your organization to compete for market share when change is introduced into your market ecosystem.

A key point to remember regarding modularity and APIs: we're not saying you should go build a bunch of APIs for everything your enterprise does. Your delivery teams are already building solutions to satisfy business demand. We are saying that when your delivery teams are building a solution for use case X, have them build it with API-based modularity for a relatively small, incremental investment.

Before moving on to the next method in the OOOps framework, one last question needs to be addressed regarding the cost of adopting a modular-by-default posture. The cost of ensuring modularity in your software delivery streams can be modeled with the same dynamics of automated deployment and automated quality testing. In any non-trivial time horizon, the return on investment is large to the point that it's only rational to treat the capital expense as an investment rather than a cost. Once your digital capability (or automated CI/CD pipeline) is used more than once, the original cost investment pays itself back in cost reduction, decreased time to value, and increased quality. This return keeps compounding with every new context of use because the original capabilities can be leveraged repeatedly (like scaled organizations use API-based capabilities to support interactions across an exploding array of channels—e.g., mobile, web, chat, phone, smart TV, etc.) without any need to rebuild redundant capabilities.

Given the industry-wide acceptance of APIs for packaging digital capabilities, creating your own version of the Bezos mandate seems incontrovertible when looking at an MVP (minimum viable product) plan. Just like the organizations that have accepted the proven value of DevOps approaches (e.g., automating pipelines for deployment and delivery), the time has come for organizations to also accept the new math and proven value of composite API infrastructures.

4

Opportunism Through Value Dynamics

I n the last chapter, you learned why it is so important to unbundle your digital assets into API-enabled business capabilities, how that approach helps you accumulate optionality in your organization, and how optionality sets the table for continuous innovation and unparalleled agility. Still, optionality is not enough on its own. To accelerate return on value, you will need to consider the business context in which your digital options can be exercised. This chapter explains and explores value dynamics, a visual approach to business context mapping. Value dynamics will improve your ability to identify high-value opportunities where you can exploit the optionality you have created through your unbundled business capabilities.

An Introduction to Value Dynamics

To apply unbundling most effectively, you need to make sure you are focusing on the right areas of your business. That means examining your business model. In the simplest definition, a business model is how your organization makes money. But that surface definition doesn't delve deeply enough into the dimensions needed for our purposes, and besides, some organizations are not about profit. A more useful definition comes from Alex Osterwalder, creator of the Business Model Canvas. He defines a business model as "the rationale of how an organization creates, delivers and captures value."[1] Following from this definition, this section focuses on how we can visually depict business models through the flow of value inside and outside an organization. Using this approach, we can more effectively vet new and existing business models, mitigate against disruptive threats, evaluate opportunities for innovation, and understand how each business capability in an organization contributes to the overall success of the business. To start to understand value dynamics, we will first look at a well-known digital success story.

Facebook generated over $70 billion of revenue in 2019,[2] but there was a time when it wasn't clear whether the social network would ever become profitable. Between 2007 and 2008, Facebook grew from twenty to 100 million users[3] but still ended up losing $150 million.[4] Conventional wisdom at the time claimed that Mark Zuckerberg had "no idea how to make money off it."[5] Given the high-profile failures of Friendster and MySpace, no one was sure whether a sustainable business model existed for social networks. This period of uncertainty, however, was short-lived. By 2010, Facebook had passed a billion dollars in annual revenue, and by 2011, a billion in annual profit.[6]

In retrospect, we can see what led to the explosive growth of Facebook from 2007–2011. Facebook's users were not paying for the service, but the personal data they provided was being monetized into advertising revenue. The Facebook developer platform launched in 2007, allowing game developers and others to build their own revenue models from which Facebook took a cut. (This "distributed innovation" strategy will be thoroughly examined in Chapter 7.) Furthermore, Facebook's modular digital architecture and infrastructure allowed the company to quickly capitalize on the mobile boom that was happening contemporaneously as well as handle its scale. Whether these steps were part of a grand plan for Facebook or whether they were happy accidents is unknown. What is known is that using a value dynamics approach ahead of time would have made it easier to see the potential payoff for each of these steps.

What Is Value Dynamics?

The complexity and interconnectedness of digital ecosystems make them difficult to navigate. As mentioned, value dynamics is a way of visually analyzing business models in an ecosystem context to develop strategies on how to intentionally evolve them. This approach builds on work done by leading thinkers in business modeling and digital ecosystems.

Peter Drucker's 1994 *Harvard Business Review* article "The Theory of the Business" is widely credited as the origin of the business model concept. In it, he describes some widely known cases of corporate disruption and claims that the cause was not complacency or inefficiency but an out-of-date set of assumptions and competencies—the business model—that defined the disrupted organizations.[7]

A few years later, Clayton Christensen's landmark book, *The Innovator's Dilemma*, delved deeply into disruptive innovation and introduced the concept of a value network as a way of providing context for an organization's business model. In Christensen's words, a value network is a "collection of upstream suppliers, downstream channels to market, and ancillary providers that support a common business model within an industry."[8] Christensen further enriched this landscape in his follow-up book, *The Innovator's Solution*, which introduced the idea of "jobs to be done." Jobs-to-be-done thinking further emphasized the notion that customers and solution providers are all part of a connected ecosystem where loyalty is fleeting and value is paramount.

With the rise of the World Wide Web and fast-growing, disruptive web-based companies, "business model innovation" arose as a trend after the turn of the millennium. Digital pirates popularized new business models: Amazon with e-commerce, eBay with online marketplaces, Google with online advertising, and Salesforce with SaaS (software as a service). Established organizations and startups alike wanted to understand the success formula these companies were using. In 2005, Alex Osterwalder and Yves Pigneur created the Business Model Canvas. This one-page, text-based tool has been widely adopted by organizations since, helping them analyze their existing business models or brainstorm new ones.

In 2001, before the Business Model Canvas came out, Jaap Gordijn and Hans Akkermans published their "e3-Value methodology," which provided a graphical method for defining business models. Written at the dawn of web business, the approach focuses specifically on value exchange between participants in digital ecosystems.[9]

Gordijn subsequently partnered with Roel Wierenga to continue refining the methodology, and they have fully articulated the approach in their recent book *Digital Business Ecosystems*. The value exchange mapping approach we use here as part of value dynamics is indebted to their work.

The Vocabulary of Value Dynamics

To define the approach, let's start by defining the key concepts of value dynamics. At the highest level, a *value network* is a bounded business eco-system within which value flows. The ecosystem consists of organizations, as well as groups of people defined by role or persona. We will refer to any of these members of a value network as *constituents*. Value networks are typically centered around a specific constituent. In our examples, we will center value networks around organizations we have discussed earlier in the book.

Constituents in a value network can deliver and capture value. A *value exchange* is the bidirectional flow of value between two constituents in a value network. Exchanged value can take many forms, from tangible to intangible. To help make value dynamics useful as an analysis and design method, we consider a discrete set of value types, or *value currencies*, as illustrated in Table 4.1.

TABLE 4.1: Value Currencies

CURRENCY	SYMBOL	DEFINITION
Money	$	Money is actual financial value exchanged between constituents.
Product		A product is value that is packaged in a form that can be possessed and used by the receiving constituent.
Service		A service is value-added work that is delivered by one constituent for the benefit of another.

Content		Content is packaged information that can be consumed by a receiving constituent, such as print or digital media.
Data		Data is encoded information that can be interpreted and synthesized to derive valuable insights.
Reach		A constituent provides reach to another by opening up access to a customer group, to a supplier network, by providing scale, and more.
Time Savings		Constituents can provide time savings through smooth user experiences, automation, aggregation, abstraction, and more.
Risk Reduction		Constituents can provide risk reduction through improved security, operation stability, insurance provision, enhanced brand equity, and more.

Facebook: A Value Dynamics Illustration

Let's demonstrate value dynamics by breaking down the flow of value in the Facebook ecosystem over time. When Facebook launched to the public in 2006, its primary value proposition was to connect individuals with each other. Users would create profiles featuring personal information and interests and then use this data to become "friends" with other users. Users found value in connecting with old acquaintances and like-minded individuals. Facebook found value in driving up its user base, a target it predicted would ultimately lead to commercial success.

Figure 4.1 shows this stage of the Facebook business model in terms of value dynamics. Users delivered data and engagement to Facebook. Facebook captured this value and used it to create new value by aggregating all users and making their personal data searchable. Facebook then delivered this "reach" back to its users, allowing them to connect and interact with each other. This approach was highly successful, as the company's user base grew from about six million to fifty million over the next year.

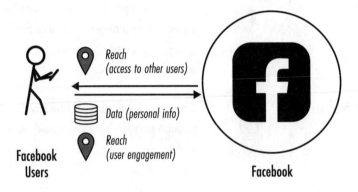

FIGURE 4.1: Value Dynamics Illustration of Facebook Business Model in 2006

Over the next few years, Facebook made a series of moves to commercialize its platform. In May 2007, Facebook opened a developer platform that allowed third parties to create applications for users to access through the social network.[10] A few months later, Facebook Ads was launched.[11] This service allowed businesses to target ads at Facebook users who could then share ad-related content with their connections. In 2009, Facebook unveiled the "Like" button, allowing users to endorse content with a single click and then have that content automatically shared with their friends.[12] In 2010, Facebook introduced its Open Graph API, which allowed anyone on the web to embed the "Like" button on their websites and engage with Facebook users through its platform.[13] These extensions to the Facebook platform significantly enhanced the Facebook business model.

As illustrated in Figure 4.2, there are new constituents in the Facebook value network. Third-party developers are now able to deliver and capture value through the Facebook developer platform and the Open Graph API. They deliver value through the apps and games they create, through websites they make shareable using the Open Graph API, and by reporting on Facebook user activity (also through the Open Graph API). Third-party businesses—another new player—pay Facebook for targeted advertising.

Revisiting the relationship between Facebook and its users, we also see new value exchanges. In addition to providing access to other users, Facebook now offers a much richer set of shared content, targeted ads, and apps and games. In exchange, users share their own content or amplify the content of others, and they may even pay for access to certain games and apps. All this increased user engagement generates more data about user activities and preferences, which Facebook uses in its ad and content targeting.

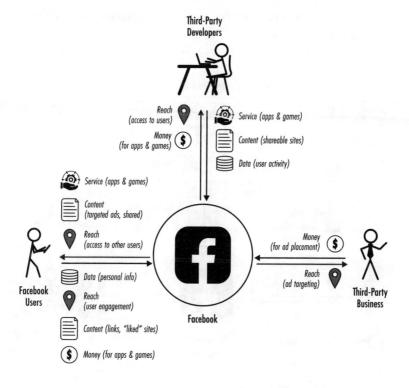

FIGURE 4.2: Facebook Business Model in 2011

This example is significant in a few ways. First, it illustrates the power of an effective platform business model, with APIs playing a significant role. Second, it emphasizes the role data can play in tilting the power balance within a value network, shown in the way Facebook collects and uses data to embolden its value exchanges. Last, and most importantly for this section, this example shows how visualizing a business model through value dynamics can provide clarity on how the model functions and where it can go next. Let's now dig into value dynamics in more detail.

Figure 4.3 shows how all the defined value dynamics concepts come together in the Facebook example. Facebook, its users, and third-party developers and businesses are the value network constituents. Each arrow depicts value being delivered by one constituent and captured by another. The icons and descriptions of value such as "money" and "data" are the different value currencies. Taken together, the set of arrows and icons that connect constituents are the value exchanges.

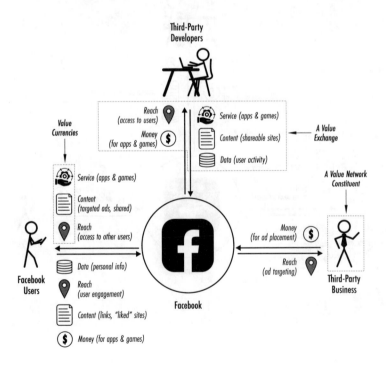

FIGURE 4.3: Value Dynamics Concepts in the Facebook Value Network

APIs as a Medium of Value Exchange

In each of the unbundling examples we discuss throughout the book, you can see how value exchanges are enabled by APIs.

- Facebook's Open Graph API allowed third-party developers to embed Facebook "Likes" on their websites as well as launch apps on the Facebook platform. It also allowed third-party businesses to engage in targeted marketing.
- Cox Automotive's Autotrader APIs (discussed in Chapter 6) allowed ecosystem partners like car makers and car sellers and ancillary players like finance providers, insurance companies, and extended warranty providers to market and sell their products to a captive audience while providing useful analytics.
- By opening its map technology through an API, Google allowed third-party businesses to integrate its geolocation services into new user experiences and contexts.
- Coca-Cola's Freestyle drink dispensers were enabled through APIs, allowing the collection of real-time operational data as well as providing personalization through its mobile app.
- Amazon Web Services' primary interface to developers is its API, and AWS is itself built on top of layers of APIs that were unbundled from core Amazon retail technology services.
- Best Buy was able to connect its Geek Squad operations to its retail stores to deliver the innovative buyback program (discussed in Chapter 9).

It is not just that APIs enabled these innovative scenarios. In each case, opening business capabilities through APIs allowed an incremental roll-out that gave the companies time to learn and adjust as they went. In the highlighted Amazon case, they were able to leverage existing API-enabled capabilities to build a whole new business unit (AWS). APIs are a powerful medium for value exchange. Now let's examine specific ways you can use value dynamics to proactively design API-enabled innovations.

Applying Value Dynamics

Harkening back to our pirate analogy, you can think about value dynamics as a way of figuring out which islands you want to target in your treasure hunt. In the digital seas, all islands may have treasure, but certain islands will yield more treasure for your business than others. Value dynamics gives you a way of divining those ones sooner and thus finding more treasure with less digging.

Value dynamics offers a framework that can enhance our comprehension of how an organization's business model fits into a larger business ecosystem and how specific business capabilities contribute to its success. By utilizing this framework, value dynamics can serve as a foundation for devising business strategies and identifying a range of potential opportunities, from making small adjustments to existing business models to introducing groundbreaking innovations. For our purposes, we especially want to consider how APIs and data can introduce and augment value exchanges to drive more innovative digital business models. Here are six ways you can use value dynamics to your advantage.

1. analyze existing business models
2. define new business models
3. find new value channels
4. augment current value exchanges
5. optimize supply-side exchanges
6. connect value networks

Analyze Existing Business Models

Value dynamics is a great tool for assessing existing business models. Using value dynamics, you can articulate your organization's value networks by determining its current customer segments and product offerings. You can then map out the constituents, value exchanges, and core business capabilities. From the resulting map, you can analyze the value network in several useful ways:

- How balanced and sustainable are the value exchanges?
- How well-differentiated are your organization's enabling capabilities?
- Are there additional value currencies that can be captured on existing exchanges?
- Are there any constituents who are positioned to disrupt the overall ecosystem?

This analysis can be done periodically as a business model health check for your organization.

Define New Business Models

You can use value dynamics to create models for new business opportunities or even to rethink your whole company's business model. Start by charting specific customer segments and how value might be exchanged between them and your organization. Include intermediaries of exchange as constituents in the value network. Consider what other constituents are supporting your organization's value delivery.

Here are some other questions to think through during this process that will help you flesh out your business model:

- What do my competitors' value networks look like?
- Are there constituents or value exchanges my organization is missing?
- What do the value networks look like for organizations in similar positions in other industries?
- Are there patterns of innovation my organization can replicate in our industry?

There are plenty of examples of companies replicating patterns from one industry into another, especially in the API economy. For example, Twilio has provided a template for "API retailing" that has been replicated by Plaid in banking and Nylas in email.

Find New Value Channels

Value dynamics can help identify missing links in your organization's value network, especially between your organization and its end customers. Successful digital companies emphasize direct customer engagement. It is vital to have a direct digital channel established for value exchange with the ultimate beneficiary of your products and services.

Ask these questions to identify new channels for value exchange in your business model:

- What are other ways my organization can reach its customers with the value it delivers?
- What value exchanges can be disintermediated?
- What value exchanges can be digitized using new channels?

The more value channels an organization creates, the more defensible its value proposition becomes.

Augment Current Value Exchanges

Value dynamics allows you to zoom in on each of your organization's value exchanges to scrutinize whether there is more value that can be captured or delivered. The creation of value exchanges is motivated by the difference in how each constituent perceives the value being exchanged. By their nature, all value exchanges are asymmetrical, in the sense that each constituent values the different currencies being exchanged differently. So, it is quite possible that there are new currencies your organization could request from its value network constituents that would increase the value you capture without having them feel like they're giving anything away.

Here are some questions to consider getting more out of your existing value exchanges:

- Is there anything my organization is capturing from value network constituents that is not currently being used to create or deliver value in the network?

- Are there any value exchanges where my organization is not cap-turing data that is being used to create value for or deliver value to other value exchanges?
- Are there any value exchanges that could be augmented through the intangible currencies of time savings, reach, or risk reduction?
- Can added trust or data transparency accelerate and enhance the exchange of value?

Augmenting existing value exchanges can offer quick wins for your business model.

Optimize Supply-Side Exchanges

Your organization may depend on other organizations to deliver its value proposition. Whether these are supplier relationships "behind" your organization in the value network or service relationships "beside" your organization, you can use value dynamics to optimize this aspect of your value network.

Here are some questions to guide your thinking in this area:

- Are there any areas where your organization is dependent on a sole supplier that could be diversified to reduce cost or risk?
- Are there suppliers or service providers that rise above their peers and warrant exclusivity?
- Are there any supplier value exchanges that could be insourced?
- Are there commoditized capabilities in your organization that could be outsourced?

Maintaining focus on core, differentiated capabilities is vital in the digital economy, something that is complemented well by optimizing partner relationships through value dynamics.

Connect Value Networks

A hallmark of digital giants like Google and Amazon is their legacy of con-necting disparate value networks through internal capability integration.

Think of Google's ad network integration into YouTube or the creation of AWS from retail infrastructure services. Organizations with diversified lines of business can map out each business unit's value network and then overlay the maps to identify opportunities for connection.

Here are some areas of consideration in taking this approach:

- What value can capabilities in one value network deliver within another?
- What data can be shared between value networks to create new value that can be delivered in one or more value networks?
- Can capabilities in one value network provide intangible value— reach, reduced risk, time savings, trust, value transparency—in another value network?

Connecting an organization's value networks can improve an organization's composite value proposition exponentially. (This will be discussed in more detail in Chapter 9.)

Finding Value

This chapter introduced the concept of value dynamics, examined real-world examples of value exchange maps, and provided methods of applying value dynamics to drive innovation. We have found value dynamics to provide a simple yet powerful perspective that suppresses unnecessary complexity and distills the essential ingredients of innovation. It's like a treasure map for digital strategy. Now let's turn to the third and final method of our science of happy accidents.

5

Optimization Through Feedback Loops

M any of the ideas and methods we explore in this book are relatively new in the context of a global economy that has been, for the most part, accelerating since the start of the Industrial Revolution. Conversely, one aspect of the OOOps methodology can be traced back to the 1880s, when Thomas Edison famously developed a working incandescent light through the process of identifying 10,000 ways the light bulb would not work.

Thomas Edison's 1882 New York electrical demonstration (referred to in Chapter 1) heralded the dawn of the electrical age. This dawn, however, was not what anyone today would call "a blink and you might miss it" moment. While it was immediately clear that the world would never be the same and the new era of the Industrial Revolution was ultimately inevitable, it took until 1927 for the electrical light to ultimately replace candles and gas lamps. In the market for electric lighting, the incandescent light bulb created by Edison was not a breakthrough product with consumers.

While Edison's light bulb did indeed create light from electricity as promised, there were several future incremental innovations and infrastructure expenditures that needed to come into being to create the space for scaled, sustained consumer demand. Lighting systems needed to be decomposed into wiring, sockets, and bulbs. Sizes and currents had to be standardized. Lighting output had to be made more efficient. One crucial innovation that enabled the mass production and adoption of electrical lighting was the result of a happy accident.

The $10,000,000 Accident

Marvin Pipkin was a lifelong tinkerer. During World War I, he went to work for General Electric at the Nela Park laboratory in Cleveland, Ohio, where he helped develop gas masks for the frontlines. Following the war, he stayed at Nela Park, devoting himself to solving a problem that had baffled the scientific community up to that point: How to produce bulbs that diffused light better than clear glass? People had attempted to create "frosted" glass bulbs by treating clear glass with acid. These bulbs improved light diffusion but introduced other problems. If the frosting process was done on the exterior, the bulbs became magnets for dust and debris. If the frosting was done on the inside, the bulbs became highly breakable.[1]

FIGURE 5.1: Headline from *Popular Science Monthly*'s August 1927 Edition
Source: Kenneth Wilcox Payne. "A $10,000,000 'Accident.'" *Popular Science Monthly*. August 1927.

Pipkin was undeterred, convinced that a durable, internally frosted light bulb was going to be the answer. Starting in 1919, Pipkin began experimenting to find the right formula, going years without success. In 1925, he accidentally overturned a batch of six frosted bulbs that were being cleaned, spilling the cleaning solution on the floor. Later, in a second accident, he knocked some of the partially cleaned bulbs onto the floor. Expecting the bulbs to shatter, he was astonished to see them bounce unbroken. He repeated the partial cleaning process, and it yielded the same result. In an authentic oops moment, Pipkin had finally discovered a way of producing durable, frosted light bulbs. In fact, his frosted bulbs turned out to be far more durable than the clear glass bulbs that were standard at the time. Within two years, Pipkin's method was adopted at scale and used to produce hundreds of millions of light bulbs.[2]

There are multiple lessons here for the digital age. First, innovation is never done. Even as organizations implement proven innovations, they must look to see what innovations come next, especially those innovations that are made possible by the ones being implemented. Second, there is a lesson in the fundamental impact of Pipkin's frosted bulb. The improved diffusion of light made it a better bulb, but it was the bulb's durability that made it a game changer, allowing it to be adopted on a massive scale. Last, there is a hidden lesson in Pipkin's six-year effort to create a light bulb suitable for massive scale. By contrast, Edison spent just over one year in the pursuit of creating a working light bulb that would not burn out in a few moments. While we don't have a time machine to observe the two tinkerers, we might not need one to understand the time difference. Edison, unlike Pipkin, had a team of forty researchers, i.e., Edison had quite a lot of shovels and a crew to dig the holes. Pipkin, on the other hand, was more like an unfortunate pirate captain who, in search of buried treasure, could only afford to dig one hole at a time.

Pipkin was not only limited by the constraint of having just two hands, but he was also limited by the constraints of the physical world, where the amount of time to execute an experiment, on real-world objects, is extremely difficult to compress. If, somehow, Pipkin was able to execute each iteration of his experiments in half the time, or if he'd had an assistant, he might have been able to find his eureka moment sooner, but given the accidental nature of his pivotal discovery, we can't really be sure. Despite our lack of certainty here, the lesson still holds—innovation is a continuous process that can be optimized! A clear catalyst to developing breakthrough innovations in any market lies in your ability to (a) compress the cycle time of your experiments or (b) execute more experiments in parallel. (This is why Bob beat Greybeard! Because Bob took on the fixed cost of making his clockwork pirates, he dropped his variable cost per hole dug down to the point where he no longer cared. Thus, he was able to use a thousand shovels and dig everywhere at once!)

The Economics of Optimizing Your Feedback Loops

In enterprises that have fully embraced both DevOps and Agile methodologies, business teams are likely to have accepted the business value of sustained commitments to delivering small changes frequently via CI/CD (continuous integration/continuous deployment). While systems thinkers are fluent in how these investments systematically drive down the cost to make and test incremental production changes, you cannot reasonably expect that everyone in your enterprise will be fully aligned with the relationship between the perceived cost to deliver a change and enterprise financial performance.

Neither Agile nor DevOps methodologies will necessarily improve enterprise financial performance when applied in isolation, but the two methods paired together can fundamentally change the enterprise itself by changing the behaviors of the people within them (with a nice fiscal impact to boot).

One path to unpack and illustrate how these two sets of practices pair together to improve organizational performance is to explore how your enterprise would be different if the cost of offering a smaller unit of value delivery were nominal or too low to notice.

When the cost to deliver change in an organization drops precipitously, a new state of "flow" will inevitably emerge within that enterprise. If all of the various stakeholders in your enterprise could schedule "urgent" changes with short lead times and low costs, would antipattern behaviors like "feature packing" (where all stakeholders try to add their entire shopping list into a sprint or release because releases are rare and the annual plan was set months ago despite not being able to predict how the market would evolve) be so common? If changes were cheap and relatively quick, would IT leaders fight over tech debt retirement? When competing interests no longer have the incentive to engage in battles over delivery capacity (i.e., who gets to decide what goes into and what gets excluded from a sprint), fusion team members have more space to deliver and less need for slide decks to justify why we have to upgrade the version of a key library in an application built by the person who left the company five years ago.

As the incremental cost to make, test, and validate a change to production systems drops, actors within an organization will cease to have the same concerns about choosing one scope item over another (because they no longer must). In other words, as the cost to make a small change falls, so does the opportunity cost of choosing one small change over another. When a new state of perceived utility arrives, value-seeking actors in the system should, by definition, ask themselves, "How many experiments or variations can I try at once in order to shorten the time to find the optimal solution?" This question gets at the heart of the change in flow within an enterprise. As the cost to deliver changes goes down, the demand (by those seeking value) to make those changes will inevitably go up.

To see this phenomenon play out in your day-to-day life, look at the photos on your phone. In the pre-smartphone world, film was expensive and the time between pressing the button and seeing the developed picture was long. In the post-smartphone world, the cost and time to value of taking a picture are basically zero. This is why your phone is full of a million and three garbage shots—because you no longer need to be conservative with how many pictures you take. Instead, you press the button to capture picture after picture to minimize the chances of missing the perfect shot.

While it may not be possible to drop the cost of change to zero, it is quite possible to drive the cost of change into a downward trend by paving the paths and roads teams must travel to understand and validate the impact of their changes in production systems (i.e., If the cost and time to understand and validate the impact of changes in production systems drops, then the cost to fully release a change to a production system must drop as well, given that the process of making a change fully includes the process of validating the impact of that change).

Minimizing the Cost of Experimentation

To see this pattern play out at scale, we must only look to concepts that were articulated by the team at Amazon over a decade ago. In Chapter 1, we saw how Amazon parallelized innovation through API-based unbundling, but it doesn't end there. In a talk at MIT where Jeff Bezos and Robert Frederick (the first product manager for AWS) talked in depth about the mechanics of a culture of innovation and experimentation, Bezos states:

> The way to get a lot of innovation in a company, in my opinion, is to work very, very hard to reduce the cost of doing experiments. Because the problem is, if experiments are expensive, then very few people are going to get to do very few experiments. That's just the way it works....It's important to reduce the cost of experimentation and then have some objective standards about what's better than what. If you can do that, then you can do a lot of innovation.[3]

As your enterprise proceeds upon the journey to become a composable enterprise capable of offering new combinations of value delivery with minimal impact on costs, it is rational to expect a rise in demand for new and different combinations to occur. Like Amazon's experience, when it's cheap to experiment with creating new offerings, many people will create many experiments, specifically because the expense is small and the risk is controllable (e.g., Captain Bob can dig one thousand holes at once because deploying the clockwork mice is cheap once he's built the fleet).

Conversely, when it's expensive to experiment, very few people will compete over who gets to run which experiment, specifically because the expense is prohibitive and the risk is uncontrollable (e.g., Captain Greybeard and his crew only dig in one or two places and often spend more time and resources fighting about where to dig than they do digging the one or two holes).

Unbundling Reduces Cycle Time

As we wind our clock forward from the early 1900s when we started this chapter, we (like the folks at AWS in the earlier example) have the luxury of working on digital experiments rather than analog ones, and it is this new laboratory that can make all the difference. In the digital world, both the cycle time of an experiment and the number of experiments you can run in parallel are fully within your control.

Over the course of the last few decades, practices from Lean, Agile, and DevOps have transformed global businesses in a host of ways. Each of these movements shares a similar core belief of small changes delivered frequently to keep the flow of value coming out of delivery teams smooth and pre-dictable. The capability of your organization to align around making small changes delivered frequently is what will make or break your ability to derive value from the options you create through modularity with APIs.

To deliver the planned benefits of optionality, we need leadership and delivery teams to look closely at the path that enterprises use to take an idea from concept to reality. Two specific aspects that you'll need to pay attention to are cycle time (the amount of elapsed time it takes for a process to complete) and the specific tactics that keep cycle time low. Focusing your resources on lowering the average cycle time of experiments within your enterprise is the most important concept in embracing optimization.

An important question to ask at this point is: Why? Why does keeping the experiment cycle time tight and the cost of experimentation low mat-ter? In fact, one might ask the same question of a Lean, Agile, or DevOps expert. Why do these methods deliver better results? Why does delivering small changes frequently matter? What's inside the methods that allow better performance to emerge?

The answer to these questions is quite simple and can be found in the work of Peter Senge. Senge rose to notoriety within the organizational devel-opment community in the 1990s with his book *The Fifth Discipline*. A key concept of Senge's work can be summed up in one of his own quotes: "The only sustainable competitive advantage is an organization's ability to learn faster than the competition."[4]

This idea answers all the previous questions. The reason enterprises that embrace delivering small change frequently outperform their competitors is because this posture allows them to learn faster and apply the learnings quicker than their competitors. The purpose of developing an ecosystem of experiments, where experiment cycle time is tight and the cost of experimentation is low, is to institutionalize the ever-accelerating path to beneficial insight.

The various strategies and techniques of creating unbundled options via APIs position organizations to thrive within the chaos of a market space by establishing an approach to delivering unpredictable innovation in a systematic way: prepare early and decide late. This optionality-based approach to innovation creates a new kind of proactivity that ultimately accelerates both the identification of exploitable opportunities and the harvesting of the uncapped gains that can come from unpredictable innovation events—happy accidents.

Like the previous two OOOps methods, this third method hasn't been restricted to digital pirates like Amazon. This method played out in a serial fashion at Anderson Holdings (discussed in detail in Chapter 7), the California-based holding company, with six subsidiaries that cut across a variety of long-established industries—automotive, real estate, insurance, and beverages. Anderson's transformation, grounded in API-based modularity and an obsession with feedback loops, yielded impressive results, including dropping the financial closing time by more than 90% and accelerating projects from weeks to hours to scale their product lines and turn four products into a hundred different combinations.

One specific requirement that we've touched on for these techniques to function and scale effectively is focusing on "cheapening the bets." For the optionality-based approach to work at a financial level, you need to be able to place many low-cost bets. To lean into this systematic approach for generating happy accidents, the adopting organization must make a commitment to keep the cost of generating, preserving, and experimenting with optionality low. Without this commitment, the environment required to yield the disproportionate benefits of a composable and interoperable enterprise can't be attained or preserved. (You'll be the pirate captain who can't afford to dig in more than one or two places at once. You may have shovels, but you don't have the mechanical crew to do the digging.)

In other words, you must consistently invest not only in creating the options themselves but also in cheapening the bets across the board. In every story and quoted excerpt throughout this book, this concept keeps recurring.

It's not just about running experiments; it's about creating the conditions in your enterprise where the variable cost of running an experiment is consistently going down. For readers who've read other books in the IT Revolution library, this should come as no surprise, as a fundamental principle espoused by leaders across Lean and DevOps circles is to keep prioritizing the system of work over doing work.

Prioritizing the Digital Systems of Work

This idea regarding a continuous focus on improving the system of work was the focus of Michael Rembetsy and Patrick McDonnell's 2012 Velocity London conference talk, "Continuously Deploying Culture." Both Rembetsy and McDonnell were leaders at Etsy at the time. For the last decade, Etsy has been perhaps the most advanced enterprise when it comes to practices of creating a culture of experimentation with a blend of business culture and automation technology.

If you read Etsy's *Code as Craft* blog, you'll find dozens of highly detailed entries on their processes and techniques to create and analyze different scenarios with live traffic from actual users. Between all the blog posts and several open-source frameworks made available by the Etsy teams, there are four main themes (as we previously mentioned in Chapter 2) that emerge for how another enterprise could take the path carved out by Etsy to deliver consumer-facing experimentation at scale:

1. **Feature flags:** The Etsy team has created (and open-sourced) a capability to make a change in consumer-facing experiences partially available to controlled sets of audiences. From the color of a screen element to an alternative copy to a change in the flow of screens for any user task, Etsy can turn these changes on or off with a single configuration commonly referred to as a feature flag.

2. **Ramps:** The size of the controlled set of audience members receiving the experimental change can be ramped up or down

as a percentage of all application traffic, again with a single configuration.

3. **Visualization:** The changes in audience behavior are all highly observable and can be instantly visualized, allowing staff to see the results of the experiment by comparing the behavior of users in the experiment and those of a control group who are not.

4. **Statistical literacy and tooling:** The business and technical teams are deeply familiar with the language and tools of statistics, allowing everyone to not only be on the same page regarding how experiments are performing but also be extremely precise in describing the results of the experiment and how those results will scale as the audience being exposed to the new code scales.

These four capabilities come together for Etsy to make the process of experimentation highly effective in terms of separating winning and losing concepts while also making the process (and variable cost) of executing an individual experiment extremely cheap. In other words, Etsy's investment in lowering the cost of experimentation has put a fleet of low-cost, drone-mounted shovels in the hands of their delivery and strategy teams. Dan McKinley, formerly of Etsy and now VP of Data, Engineering, and Operations for Mozilla, lays out how in a post on his blog titled "Design for Continuous Experimentation."[5]

Before leaving the tools aspect of how to lower the cost of experiments, let's look at Etsy's work through the lens of the OOOps framework. The capabilities to run experiments demonstrated at Etsy are focused in the market interface layer between the Etsy store and the user (where a user can be either a buyer or a seller). While Etsy's *Code as Craft* blog is full of fascinating examples of scaled experimentation capabilities, what we don't see is any content about performing these types of experiments with packaged SaaS offerings based on APIs that decontextualize the digital capabilities Etsy made to optimize their own experiences.

To make this distinction easily understood, let's compare Amazon with Etsy here. Amazon understood how advanced their infrastructure capabilities were and how enterprises of all types would want to consume their infrastructure as a service. This capability came to market (generally speaking) as AWS.

Etsy's feature-testing capabilities, described above, are talked about and even shared as open-source code for consumers to use as they choose, but Etsy has not made their experimentation capabilities available as a paid SaaS offering that any enterprise user could consume without having to make larger investments in infrastructure and scaling.

In other words, Etsy has created a mechanism to cheapen its bets at the storefront level but has not fully unbundled and externalized its capabilities to make it possible to offer decontextualized capabilities to other enterprises that might find these capabilities valuable. (This choice by the leadership team at Etsy, and the choice by the team at Amazon, is a business and market strategy question. We'll take a closer look at this decision in Chapter 8.)

While the tooling available at Etsy is impressive and compelling (especially for 2012), it is important to remember that advanced tools are only one leg of the stool that includes people (a team well-versed in statistical literacy) and processes. It is also important to note that three of the four capabilities that Etsy used to continually optimize its e-commerce marketplace are all available from various vendors (discussed in more detail in Chapter 8) and open-source communities. The fourth capability (a team and culture grounded in statistical literacy) can be acquired with a mix of process discipline, training, and hiring.

Regarding the need for process discipline, many scaled organizations have neither codified nor optimized the stages of a digital experiment. This is a major and distinct gap that prevents these organizations from being able to leverage, or even perceive, the benefits of optionality. The framework we present in Figure 5.2 isn't meant to be the definitive model for creating an ecosystem of experimentation. Think of it as a reasonable starting point that can be used if your organization hasn't yet aligned to a formal model.

Historical learning strategies for enterprises often speak to "mean time to insight" as the cycle to compress. In the last fifteen years, specific advances in technology have made it possible to go one step further and compress the cycle all the way through the adaptation that can be created because of the insight.

Just as DevOps principles help an organization "shift left" and compress specific steps in the SDLC (software development life cycle) to observe and remediate quality issues, the tactics to develop and preserve optionality within your enterprise will help you shift left and compress the time from "envisioning to adapting."

FIGURE 5.2: A Life Cycle Model for Digital Experiments

In another parallel to how consumer-grade lighting solutions evolved, scaled optionality only became accessible by enterprises around the world through a series of incremental innovations. It is only in recent times, with the democratization of scaled cloud technologies, that significant gains from optionality can be attained by both digital pirates and settlers alike. As shown in Figure 5.3, the context we are in now is one where multiple advances are sufficiently understood by a wide enough community that all enterprises can take full advantage of them.

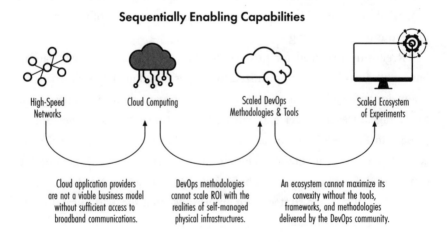

FIGURE 5.3: Evolutionary Advancements Toward Scalable Optionality

Systematizing Innovation

This chapter explored the last of the three OOOps methods: optimizing through feedback loops. At this point, it is important to note that each of the three OOOps methods is insufficient on its own to create the scaled fiscal impact that the digital pirates have achieved. It is only through using them in concert that enterprises will reap the rewards of preparing early so you can decide later.

Within Part I of this book, we have presented actionable methods for applying the unbundling techniques pioneered by the digital pirates.

- API-based **optionality** creates an organizational well-spring of opportunities with the type of high-margin potential that isn't limited to the digital pirates. The "new financial math" explained in Chapter 3 can help you measure the right things and align your organization to make these opportunities more financially viable.
- Value dynamics creates a new game board for developing a digital strategy that helps to identify gaps in existing business models as well as **opportunities** for innovation and optimization.
- Establishing and **optimizing** feedback loops and communication channels throughout your business will allow you to pounce on opportunities and correct issues at the right time.

Adopting these methods and using them in concert will help take your transformation efforts to the next level.

Now that we've established the methods of scaled unbundling, we're ready to examine how these methods can be combined and leveraged to execute the four treasure-hunting strategies enumerated in the introduction—exchange optimization, distributed innovation, capability capitalization, and value aggregation.

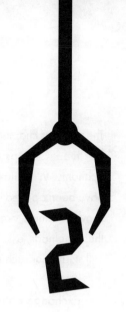

SUCCESS STRATEGIES

The previous chapters showed how organizations utilized new methods—the three OOOps methods—to find sustained success in the digital economy. In the next four chapters, we will explore how these methods have been applied in detail by these organizations. Specifically, we will show how these organizations are applying practical strategies through these methods, essentially running plays from a common playbook. We will study four such strategies:

- **Exchange optimization:** Adapting and evolving old business models to the digital world, with a focus on speeding up processes, augmenting customer experiences, and lowering operating costs.
- **Distributed innovation:** Turning customers, partners, and non-technical colleagues into digital innovators by providing tools and incentives to experiment and build on a constrained and instrumented platform.
- **Capability capitalization:** Repurposing digital capabilities from one part of the business to create new products and services in other business units or through other channels.
- **Value aggregation:** Combining value streams from different parts of the business to create a composite business model whose value is greater than the sum of its parts.

We have derived these four success strategies from actual examples that have been proven through both digital pirates and digital settlers. These are not the only strategies for digital success, but studying how they work may help you identify additional ones. Let's now investigate each of the strategies, the case studies that illustrate them, and how the three methods in the science of happy accidents have been used to realize them.

6

Strategies of Success #1: Exchange Optimization

I n this chapter, we will take a close look at the first of four unbundling success strategies: *exchange optimization*. In this strategy, organizations use the OOOps methods to adapt linear and isolated business models for an interconnected digital ecosystem. They use APIs not only as the connection points between systems but, more importantly, as the lubricant between business models. API-based modularity can enhance the speed and scale of a value exchange while also lowering coordination costs for all the exchange participants.

To demonstrate the strategy, we will show how digital hybrid Cox Automotive (a multi-brand organization that has been built by acquisition from a mix of both pirates and settlers) assembled more than fifty independent automotive ecosystem businesses and transformed them into an interconnected platform. As a "house of brands," Cox Automotive may not be as recognizable as several of its lines of business, which include Autotrader and Kelley Blue Book, but Cox Automotive is a $7 billion independent organization inside of Cox Enterprises, which is one of the fifteen largest private companies in the United States. Cox Automotive's offerings help to remove friction from an automotive economy that represented almost 5% of the US GDP and employed almost ten million Americans in 2022.[1] We'll also look at two digital settlers—Lowe's and L Brands—that reinvented their operating models by optimizing their value exchanges both inside and out.

Outside of the OOOps methods, these stories highlight the critical importance of both grounding and aligning your API-based efforts with the needs of sales and financial leadership. Knowing that you might be engaged with the financial leadership of your enterprise, we first need to gear up and explore how finance sees the world.

You Can't Beat Finance...So Join Them

In talking with leaders around the globe, there was an unsurprising unanimity among them. Whether they came from digital pirates or digital settlers, they had a common point of view. Even the leaders within public sector organizations espoused the same perspective on a critical success factor. In your efforts to drive your enterprise to embrace an unbundled future full of convex options, finance will either be the friction or the flywheel to your success. This is largely due to the nature of how almost every organization classifies and treats cost centers versus revenue centers (or public value centers in the context of public sector organizations).

Finance, business, and technical leaders alike, regardless of geography or industry, see businesses and the activities within them as a series of models. The traditional classification model of cost centers and revenue centers (shown in Figure 6.1) breaks down when you recognize that most scaled organizations have some type of operations teams embedded within each of the teams classified as revenue centers.

Legacy Cost vs. Revenue Organization Models

FIGURE 6.1: Cost vs. Revenue Centers

The reductive model of cost activities versus revenue activities has been problematic for both digital pirates and settlers, but a trend from the last decade shows a path to a more harmonious and productive organization. This is achieved by sidestepping the classifications that beg adversarial conflict within an organization: federating and dedicating operational roles within delivery and product teams (e.g., DevOps, RevOps, FinOps, etc.). The Ops suffix trend that started with DevOps isn't confined to technical disciplines like software development, application infrastructure, and cybersecurity. This newer posture reduces inter-team conflict by embedding the operational responsibilities within each team rather than allowing an upstream team to pass risk downstream to a different team that must carry the risk while having no decision-making power to mitigate or avoid the risk.

The rise of this new model has accelerated in the last few years in part due to a pithy phrase popularized at Amazon: "You build it, you run it." First noted in a 2006 interview with Amazon CTO Werner Vogels,[2] the phrase has significantly influenced organizational design beyond its original intent, which was, for the most part, confined to software development. Vogels's intention is clear and concise when he states, "Giving developers operational responsibilities has greatly enhanced the quality of the services, both from a customer and a technology point of view."[3] Integrating operational responsibilities into the teams responsible for value creation is aligned with a cornerstone of Amazon culture: an obsession with feedback loops. Vogels goes on to state that this operational principle brings developers "...into day-to-day contact with the customer. This customer feedback loop is essential for improving the quality of the service."[4]

This shift toward multidisciplinary "fusion teams" is popular among digital pirates, because making teams responsible for their own operational management acts as a forcing function both to keep teams honest on being efficient with their resources and to have them continually looking for ways to optimize the processes involved within their value-creating activities.

As shown in Figure 6.2, this different way of modeling the enterprise recognizes that all teams and departments consume enterprise resources (costs) *and* produce value for consumers.

Transformed Cost + Value Organization Models
All Departments

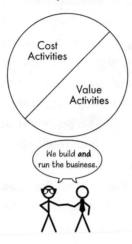

FIGURE 6.2: Cost + Value Centers

Achieving a balance between the various types of activities is a nev-er-ending challenge in most organizations, given that the typical objectives shift and change based on a chaotic marketplace. In times of rapid growth, leaders will often call for a near-term mindset of capturing market share at the expense of optimal operating posture. Conversely, in times of disruption, a compression mindset can take over, where all cost centers must find ways to do more with less despite not having financial resources to improve oper-ational productivity ratios. While the ratio of cost to consumer value may be different for each team, the ratio is typically changeable through automation, optimization, and achieving scale by increasing labor capacity.

Given that cost-versus-value culture in most organizations isn't likely to change anytime soon, a leader who wants to transform their organization's approach to modularity, APIs, and optionality will have to chart a course to support efforts to unbundle capabilities without having a well-understood path to revenue.

Finding this course is a common struggle among both digital pirates and settlers. Of the organizations we researched in the development of this book, one brings unique insight into building shared capabilities while not attracting financial scrutiny: Cox Automotive.

Cox Automotive Carves Its Own Road

Cox Automotive has both the legacy of physical marketplaces from Manheim Auctions (the leading automobile auction provider in the United States) and the digital skills necessary to run high-profile web properties like Autotrader and Kelley Blue Book. Cox Auto's unique heritage crosses the physical and digital worlds, giving its technology leaders distinct and powerful insight into the nature of transformation.

Cox Automotive's parent company, Cox Enterprises, created the site Autotrader through an intentional cannibalization of its diverse media businesses when local newspapers, radio, and TV advertising began to show signs of decline. Cox Enterprises grew to scale as a media conglomerate and, to the surprise of many, made its entry into the automotive ecosystem with the purchase of Manheim Auctions.

When Cox bought Manheim in 1968, some people wondered why a media empire was getting into the automotive business. James Cox Jr. was attracted to Manheim using the characteristics—customer service, high margins, and growth potential—that had been passed down to him from his father, James, who had founded Cox Enterprises before leaving the business to pursue a political career.

Through Manheim, the automotive industry became a great success for Cox through the 1970s and 1980s. With the dawn of the World Wide Web in the 1990s, Cox was able to combine its expertise in media and communications with its automotive acumen to launch Autotrader.com in 1999. This website provided data on car values and sales that allowed buyers to be more confident in their purchases and dealers to manage their sales more efficiently. In this way, Autotrader.com improved the availability and flow of information to people, leading to greater outcomes for both buyers and dealers.

In retrospect, Cox Enterprises' move into the automotive space seems to be an earlier analog to Amazon's move into cloud computing services. Rather than stay in its media lane, Cox found a match between customer needs and its own core competencies. The launch of Autotrader.com took this a step further, leveraging Cox Enterprises' core capabilities in media in combination with its newer understanding of automotive remarketing.

Cox Automotive Makes the Media the Message

While the internet has injected change across every industry and spawned entirely new business models, one industry has been subjected to more internet-driven volatility than perhaps any other—news media. Newspapers, and even journalism itself, have been subjected to a level of change akin to the horse and buggy at the introduction of the combustion engine. Let's look at this industry and the changes thrust upon it through the lens of value dynamics.

When we draw out the value exchanges in Cox Media's (a twentieth-century newspaper, radio, and local television empire) early business model, the ecosystem looks like the diagram in Figure 6.3.

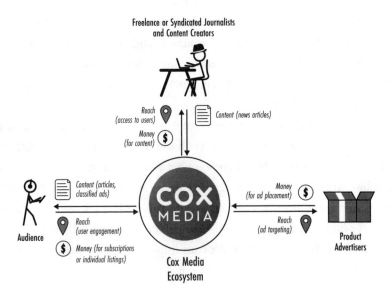

FIGURE 6.3: A Traditional Media Business Model Depicted Through Value Exchanges

The newspapers and radio and television programs deliver value to customers in the form of content, and media channels capture money in return. On the other side, the media channels provide value to advertisers in the form of exposure to their audiences and capture even more money. The final value exchange is between the newspaper and freelance journalists they might hire, giving them money and exposure in return for exclusive content. This business model was highly useful in the pre-digital age when access to content was scarcer.

Cox Media Group was founded in 2008 when its parent company, Cox Enterprises, consolidated its existing media subsidiaries across publishing, radio, and television. In a brief ten-year period, everything about the newspaper and advertising businesses changed, ultimately resulting in Cox Enterprises packaging and selling off most of its Cox Media assets.

It was during this period of accelerated change that the pieces of Cox Automotive were assembled and integrated through a mix of home-grown innovation and acquisition. There were several maneuvers that foreshadowed these two eventualities. One set of events came through the founding of Autotrader.com. Today, Autotrader is the preeminent automotive marketplace in the US. Of particular interest here is the fact that Autotrader cannibalized what was one of, if not the largest, sources of revenue for Cox Media's newspaper business: classified ads for used cars.

As shown in Figure 6.4 (see page 90), the Autotrader value ecosystem expanded upon the basic premise of classified ads for used cars and became the high-margin cornerstone that ultimately allowed for the formation of Cox Automotive.

At the time of its founding, there may have been some concern regarding why Cox would essentially compete with itself, but in today's landscape of copycats and me-toos (e.g., Cars.com, CarGurus.com, TrueCar, and others), the move to unbundle itself looks like sheer genius.

Launching Autotrader.com also demonstrated that Cox was not afraid to disrupt its own properties. Today, Cox Automotive is a thriving enterprise that combines Manheim, Autotrader, and more integrated acquisitions like industry-leading auto information provider Kelley Blue Book.

Cox's growth trajectory has come from pursuing acquisitions and cross-brand leverage points that can be exploited to increase customer engagement and wallet share. APIs and decomposition have acted as the foundation to make this strategy possible, but it has taken more than a decade to unlock and integrate the cross-brand capabilities specifically because of the siloed financial structure of the various brands.

While the process of fully transposing the disconnected business models has taken more than a decade, Cox Auto hasn't veered from its plan to be the most robust automotive ecosystem grounded in interchangeable capabilities that can operate seamlessly with one another.

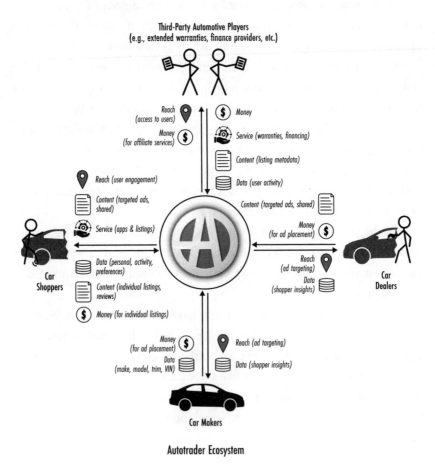

FIGURE 6.4: Autotrader Business Model Depicted Through Value Exchanges

In a recent interview, Chris Dillon, VP of Architecture and Engineering Enablement at Cox, stated:

> What we're really focused on today is composability. It's sort of the notion that instead of building these stove-piped products that don't integrate well with one another, we're extracting kind of the core capabilities and rendering them either as APIs, as sets of embeddable and composable UIs, and then stitching those products or new experiences together. That's really our vision...it's a platform for the industry of digital building blocks that can be stitched together and reconfigured in different ways.[5]

The potential of becoming a modular toolset that can act as a next-generation plug-and-play ERP (enterprise resource planning) platform for automotive dealers has been the driving motivation to form Cox Automotive and embark on a multiyear acquisition and integration journey. Only in hindsight has it become clear that the barrier to achieving the potential value for all the stakeholders was more grounded in financial and operating structure than in the tech stacks and application infrastructure. What started as small, cross-brand experiments has now become the predominant model for growth, and Cox Auto is on the path to digitize, optimize, and scale value exchanges across the entire life cycle of millions of automobiles.

While the diagram in Figure 6.4 illustrates how value flows in the Autotrader.com context, this localized view is but the beginning of how all Cox Automotive business units collaborate to transform the process of buying, selling, and owning automobiles.

A partial view of Cox Automotive's evolved ecosystem is pictured in Figure 6.5 (see page 92). A car dealer shopping for used car inventory at a Manheim auction can now buy with confidence based on the pricing analytics from vAuto. They also have the capability to utilize all the cross-brand capabilities once the auctioneer bangs the gavel. Whether it's scheduling delivery with Ready Logistics, managing their financial leverage with NextGear Capital, advertising the car on Autotrader and Kelley Blue Book, or leveraging any of the dozens of ancillary services, the buyer can start marketing and even reselling the car to their customers before the car even leaves the auction lane.

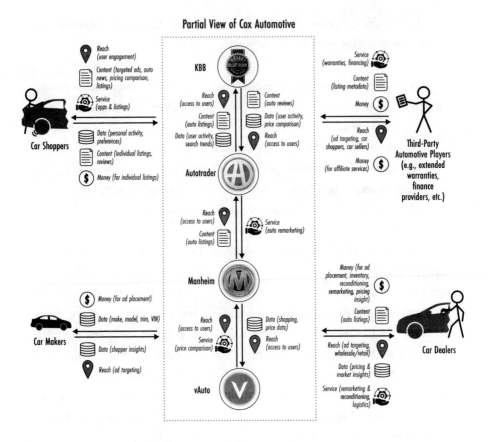

FIGURE 6.5: Partial View of Cox Automotive Ecosystem

Design with Disruption in Mind

With deep, pre-digital roots—Cox starting in 1898, Kelley Blue Book in 1918, Manheim in 1945—Cox Automotive stands as a remarkable story in digital transformation. Going beneath the surface of the company, it's clear that this is no accident. A key player in the current leadership team of Cox Automotive is David Rice, SVP of Product and Engineering.

In talking with us, Rice explained his perspective on the struggle regarding financial investments that are targeted to advance modularity, shared platforms, and integration strategies within organizations by grounding the conversation in finance concepts rather than APIs or technology:

> It's all about the S-curve of growth...You start, you grow exponentially, and then you start to idle. Companies struggle with really recognizing that they're at the top of the S-curve. When you're at the top of the S-curve, sometimes you actually have to be willing to step down in your total revenue because you can potentially get more EBITDA [earnings before interest, taxes, depreciation, and amortization] or you can use that investment to restart that S-curve and go up again.[6]

Rice has been through every phase of the S-curve that defines modern enterprises. (An S-curve represents the natural rhythm of growth, following a pattern of discovery, inflection, scaling, and inevitably decay.) He's seen small and big, new and old, acquired and acquirer, disruptor and disrupted. In each of these contexts, Rice has kept a close hand on the common API infrastructure, which he refers to as the engine of value creation. When he talks of his experiences, it's less of a recounting of personal history as it's a lesson in enterprise dynamics and the forces that drive organizational change and maturation.

In our interview, Rice expanded on the challenges business leaders experience in the transformational journey, stating:

> It's way harder in the business. The technology is hard...don't get me wrong...but it's well-defined. It's the difference between simple and easy. We're finding the enterprise product platform functionality is relatively simple, but it is not easy to implement. It's not easy to get buy-in. It's not easy to get people to take their eye off the moment of growing this one asset as much as they can and think about...we're looking to lift up everything and not just one product. This is not the technology...this is not [about] how you decompose it, how you strangle it out and replace them. This is about how do you get the business to focus on walking away from revenue in the goal of eventually getting more revenue?[7]

Rice came into Cox Automotive with the acquisition of API-driven upstart vAuto, which serves critical market data to car dealers participating in automotive auctions, where dealers and automotive financing enterprises buy and sell inventory to the tune of $3 billion in revenue for Manheim. Soon after the acquisition of vAuto, Cox continued its acquisition spree in an aim to provide a one-stop shop for products and services necessary to run a car dealership in North America. Cox Automotive doubled in size when it completed the acquisition of Dealertrack, the leader in the dealership management software market.

In the ever-changing organizational context that is his career journey, Rice's takeaway is a little different from the organizational dogma that most software executives live by: Conway's Law. Conway's Law states that organizations that design systems are constrained to produce designs that are copies of the communication structures of these organizations.[8] Rather than speak to the inevitability of Conway or the cleverness of niche strategies like the Inverse Conway Maneuver (a practice of designing your organization's communication structures to influence technical architecture decisions), Rice's take starts with more of a philosophical perspective:

> All org designs suck, and really all you're doing with an org design is you're focusing your org design, whether it's centralized or decentralized or connected to the product. You're focusing it on a set of problems that you have in this moment. But what is more important than your org design is the remediations you put in place to deal with the fact that the org design is suboptimal in a bunch of other cases.[9]

Rice observes that the business processes that were borrowed from the early digital age are the primary hindrance today:

> For twenty years it was the tech that was the hindrance. How do we get stuff fast enough to users, to consumers, to other businesses? How do we deal with the complexities of the data, the APIs, the connectivity? Those things are just the work now, but it's the business hurdles that seem to be the things that prevent you from really accelerating.[10]

Rice goes even further when he speaks about the difference between simple and easy. He states that the path technology teams must walk is simple because the tools and methods are well-defined, but the path is not easy. It requires business and culture change, which is where the real complexities lie, given that the technology execution work is well-defined, but the business modeling and design decisions are not.

Rice has emerged from the constant turmoil of an industry rife with acquisitions and disruption with a set of principles and models that he now applies reflexively. His approach to organizational models and the cycles of change they go through is less about the rationalistic lens of what will be the most efficient manner of structuring an enterprise and more about the realistic view of where power lies: in finance and revenue.

Unlike the leaders who've scaled tech unicorns and look at technology and platforms as the center of value creation, Rice lives in a world of old-school business models that are trying to ingest and harness the value of new tech-centric models through an M&A (merger and acquisition) process. After being on both sides of the M&A coin (the acquired and the acquirer), Rice has come to a series of epiphanies that have shaped not only his worldview but also his decision-making processes for how to structure organizations and enable the sustainability of iterative technology investment that will often become the focus of cost-control and compression efforts in a complex and ever-changing environment.

Where tech leaders from digital pirates to digital settlers have focused on Conway's Law for organizational change, Rice has instead focused on the distributed behaviors of business teams and executives and developed an approach that mitigates suboptimal organizational decision-making. In short, Rice has chosen a path that, due to the nature of how finance and business leaders view the world, assumes that decisions will inevitably skew to localized optimization at the expense of the whole, no matter what. Thus, the only decision left is to harness the kingdom-building behavior of business leaders by "placing value creation as close to revenue generation as possible."[11]

Rice explains that this model starts with two clashing ideas that are simultaneously true:

1. "The old way forces everything into a cost model. You know what companies do with cost? They cut them."[12]
2. Modularity, or optionality through unbundling, is the best hedge to "manage the unpredictability of the future. You have to do that early and you have to be willing to pay for that because time to market and future planning are opposing forces."[13]

In other words, it's easy to optimize for time to market for the first version of an offering but, by definition, that's not the strategy that easily scales when an offering is successful. When Rice joined his second startup, he intentionally switched the default decision-making model. He prepared for an uncertain future by establishing a set of architectural rules for embracing modularity while keeping technical debt under tight control and then positioning shortcuts (deviations that might improve speed to market by sacrificing modularity and incurring technical debt) as the exceptions that needed more scrutiny and justification. With this new operating paradigm, he made the choice to preserve optionality as the default habit for the entire delivery organization. What he found was that it was easier to execute the exceptions in this posture.

Comparatively, when a shortcut is taken, the exceptions will inevitably have lead times, complexity, and opportunity costs that are so onerous they're almost insurmountable. This barrier to the tractability of exceptions gets steeper every day as the "shortcut by default posture" is always adding more barriers to flexibility with every choice made.

For example, imagine Google had sacrificed modularity to get its Maps product to market sooner. This "shortcut" may or may not have accelerated their path to market, but with hindsight that includes the not-so-happy ending for Google Plus that chose to forgo modularity, we can say that this would have scuttled all other high-value options and made the prospect of reengineering the platform to allow for unforeseen use cases a fool's errand.

The problems of "shortcut by default" are not limited to the digital settlers. We've seen the pattern play out within many of the digital pirates as well, where the accrued technical debt becomes a balloon payment that slows all delivery to a crawl. One of the most notable cases of this antipattern occurred at LinkedIn, where the balloon payment came due and forced LinkedIn to institute a full "feature freeze" across all their products for almost a year until the debt accrued from technical shortcuts was addressed and eliminated from the application infrastructure.[14]

After living through multiple turns of the acquisition cycle, along with navigating cycles of disruption from startups dead set on cleaving off a piece of the enterprise's business, Rice's nuanced posture emerged like he was the captain of a ship charting a course through turbulent waters. Adrift in a storm whose volatile waves have the capacity to capsize the whole craft and leave the crew without life preservers to hold on to.

Rice's perspective maps back to academic research synthesized in the Safety Boundary Model, developed by Jens Rasmussen and Dr. Richard Cook (shown in Figure 6.6). Originally developed and published to describe how the operating point of manufacturing and health systems constantly moves because of experiments to optimize the systems, the framework was discovered to apply to almost every scaled system. It is frequently referenced in DevOps circles in an effort to avoid systemic risk and operational incidents.

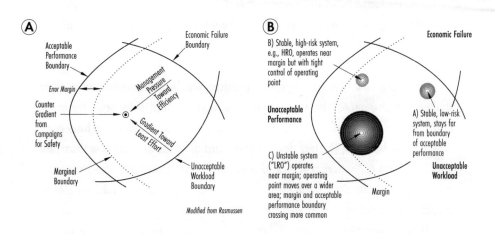

FIGURE 6.6: Safety Boundary Model

Source: J. Bradley Morrison and Robert L. Wears. "Modeling Rasmussen's Dynamic Modeling Problem: Drift Towards a Boundary of Safety." *Cognition, Technology & Work* 24, no. 1 (April 28, 2021): 127–145. https://doi.org/10.1007/s10111-021-00668-x.

What Rice describes in his efforts to protect the centers of value creation is a bet against the gradients of management pressure toward efficiency and least effort. When an inevitable, and yet unexpected, moment of economic disruption occurs, a chain of events is set in motion to preserve the economic viability of the enterprise (shown in Figure 6.7). If, in the moment of disruption,

> common services are separated from business leaders that care the most about it, it becomes a cost center. There's no skin in the game from the business side and the shared service skews to the ivory tower...We want the tech teams to feel the pain of the business and the business teams to see the commons as the engine of value creation.[15]

Rice goes further and explains,

> Even if business leaders understand the value versus the cost center mentality, you have to recognize that business leaders don't stay in place.... Meaning [you should] always be proving and keep your commons teams [e.g., the teams building APIs and other shared services] close to the highest EBITDA revenue [in order to buffer them from the unyielding waves of market volatility].[16]

Knowing that the pressure to optimize will undoubtedly come, Rice makes the proactive choice to hedge against unstoppable organizational compression by sacrificing potential efficiency in organizational architecture, which most business leaders don't understand or value anyway. We illustrate this in Figure 6.7 where a series of four sequential states is moved through when a financially disruptive event occurs, and business leadership reacts to return the company to a financially healthy context.

If the compression cycle is fundamentally inevitable given the nature of business and economic cycles, Rice has developed a proactive mitigation strategy to position key delivery teams out of the center of core-IT operations (where shared platforms usually live in scaled organizations) and closer to the edge (where revenue is harvested from value events). In this model, when finance teams look for areas to cut and compress expenses, the critical teams delivering long-term optionality and value creation are not directly in the crosshairs.

In Rice's financial-volatility-centric model, he places common functionality (like API development and platform engineering) that everyone is going to use as organizationally close as possible to the revenue that benefits from it the most. The main reason is that the primary revenue beneficiary of the shared capabilities will also be your primary stakeholder who, in the event of a financially disruptive event, will push back against finance when they're looking across the enterprise for costs to cut.

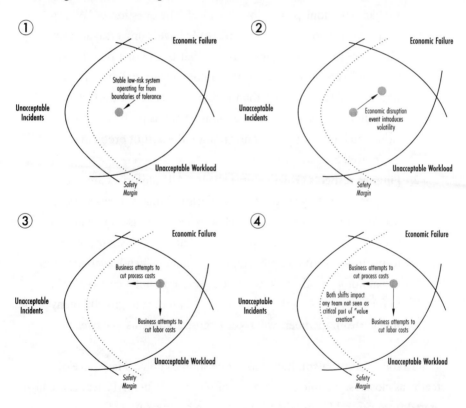

FIGURE 6.7: Adapted Boundary Model with Disruption and Response

"It's kinda backward, if you think about it," Rice states. "You buy a bunch of companies, and you want them to work together, but there are inherent hurdles in place that prevent them from working together unless they were products that were built with that in mind. In today's day and age, new products tend to need a little more of a fluid system."[17] Whether Rice is referring to the fluidity needed in the organizational and system architectures or the unending fluidity of market conditions, he's not wrong. He's focused on being one step ahead of the future.

For a more concrete example, let's take a deeper look at how Rice explains two critical concepts that set the stage for his solution.

1. **All organizational models are flawed:** Organizational models are like cell phone plans. None are ideal. The question of "What's the best cell phone plan?" doesn't really have a universal answer. The more productive question is "What cell phone plan is best for you?" What this means is that all organizational models have serious problems. Rather than trying to choose the perfect one, the better path is to choose the model that has problems that are either irrelevant for your context or are the sort of problems that you're well prepared to mitigate.

2. **Finance respects growth above all else:** All enterprises are in one of three contexts: growth, stasis, or decline. Finance treats stasis as decline. Furthermore, growth below expectations is also treated as decline. When a business unit is in decline, finance starts pushing teams to work on compressing cost centers. When leaders try to explain other truths ("IT is a value generator, not a cost center!") to finance regarding the need to invest to return to growth, many finance team members will receive those arguments as naive.

To solve this problem, Rice makes one simple choice. Place development teams as close as possible to the point of revenue. When API teams are liberated from central IT and distributed within business units that are directly associated with revenue generation, the leaders of business teams become more familiar with the value that comes out of engineering. This appreciation forestalls any compression narratives that might come from finance to force teams into the short-term decision-making that is the beginning of a downward spiral of self-fulfilling prophecies.

Rather than sussing out a method to deliver a bullet-proof ROI formula for ensuring top-down support for his plans to embed composability as a nonnegotiable concept for the engineering teams, Rice steers in the other direction. Knowing that disruption is inevitable, Rice designs his organization to thrive regardless of the chaotic changes that might come from market disruption and calls for short-term wins above all else, even the shiny baubles that other executive leaders might latch on to.

To make this concept real, let's contrast three different development organization topologies:

Traditional Enterprise IT: IT teams are segmented from and have a transactional relationship with business teams, often described in terms of who owns "the what" (what gets built) versus who owns "the how" (the technical specifications, methods for how things get built). In many traditional enterprises, integration teams are co-mingled with API teams and considered part of "back office operations" that are a cost of doing business. This organizational model is optimized for hierarchy with clean distinctions on roles and responsibilities.

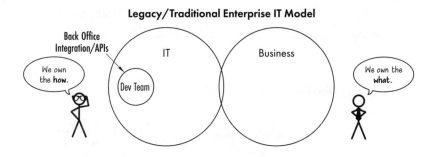

FIGURE 6.8: Traditional Enterprise IT

Stream Aligned: Sometimes called fusion teams, stream-aligned teams are multidisciplinary teams that pull together all the required skills to design, create, and operate a value stream. This type of model (explained in depth in *Team Topologies* by Matthew Skelton and Manuel Pais) is optimized for flow and widely accepted by analyst communities like Gartner and Forrester to be state of the art. While stream-aligned teams themselves can be seen as value creators, they still often rely on a centralized platform team that is charged with enabling the individual stream-aligned teams.

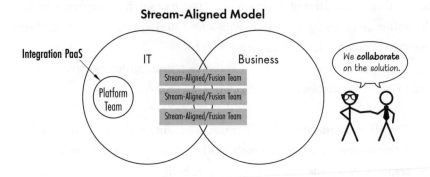

FIGURE 6.9: Stream-Aligned Model

Business Centric: Utilizing Rice's perspective, API product teams are integrated into business contexts as far as possible. This "closer to the point of value creation" model is optimized for stability when financial disruption inevitably occurs, setting up a "shock absorber" to help your organization thrive in a time of perceived uncertainty.

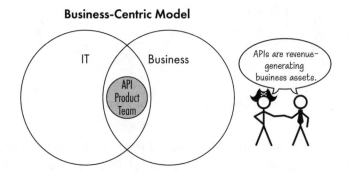

FIGURE 6.10: Business-Centric Model

Each of these models can be spread across a continuum that stratifies the difference between "cost centers" and "value creators" as shown in Figure 6.11.

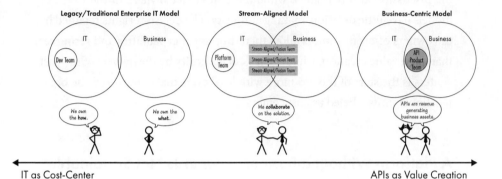

FIGURE 6.11: Cost/Value Continuum

Taking this perspective one step further, we can contrast the likely view of finance executive behavior when a financial disruption occurs:

1. **Traditional enterprise IT teams seen as a cost center:** In the event of a financial disruption, all teams seen by finance as cost centers are at high risk of deep cutbacks (i.e., finance leaders bring out the chainsaw to dramatically cut operational expenses).

2. **Stream-aligned teams seen as a partial cost center:** While not as exposed as teams perceived as "back office," platform teams that support stream-aligned teams are also at risk of finance-driven cutbacks in the event of a financial disruption (i.e., finance leaders bring out the hatchet to make cutbacks in underperforming areas).

3. **Business-centric teams seen as value creators:** When API teams are positioned as close to high-margin revenue as possible, finance reactions to disruptions are characterized as fine-tuning or reinvestment (i.e., finance leaders bring out both a scalpel and reinvestment capital to optimize value creation).

When looking at the last of the three models, it is important to note that the perceptions and reactions by finance really haven't changed. The difference in result is more a function of the fact that the profit center owners drive the discussion and decisions, while the cost center owners in the first two models have little decision-making authority. The decision rights retained by the owners of profit centers allow them to protect capabilities and resources that drive value creation, while the lack of authority by the owners of the cost centers is the start of the "do more with less" cycle that compresses the organizational units labeled as cost centers.

A Platform Without a Business Owner Is Not Sustainable

One question the business-centric model above begs is whether there's ever a safe place for platform teams to exist. On the one hand, readers of *Team Topologies* and those who work on platform teams may say it's a fundamental need if an enterprise wants to sustainably compete in the fast-paced world of software. On the other hand is the pragmatist perspective of finance-driven enterprises that the current times, abundant with disruption (even for the Big Tech companies), tell us can't be denied.

We directly asked this question to Rice, and he deftly unpacked a more fluid idea based on the perspectives of business leaders when it comes to platforms and platform economics.

As shown in Figure 6.12, when IT is driving the conversation on platforms and organizing around them outside of a business context, like the platform as an IT-owned concept on the left, that's a good sign you're on a path that isn't going to end well. When platforms become the organizational strategy, like the context in the middle of the continuum, or one step further on the right, or become the specific "business-owned product" that has materialized into reality, it's more likely to be a path that can withstand the disruption that will inevitably come.

This continuum and the states within it are not related to platform or IT maturity. Instead, this continuum is driven by business maturity and acceptance of the financial opportunities associated with digital products and platforms. Additionally, this model doesn't necessarily mean that technology leaders would be wise to never engage in platform development or socialize platform concepts and initiatives with business leaders. Instead, this model illustrates the path digital settlers rather than pirates must walk to make any sustainable change.

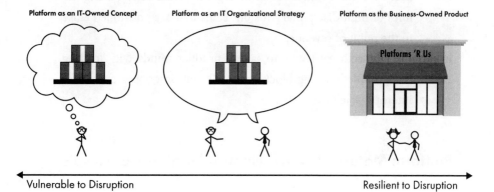

FIGURE 6.12: IT vs. Business-Owned Platforms

Transformation and platforms must be grounded in outcomes that the business teams own. Until such time as business leaders orient and align on platforms as springboards to a new future, attempting to force this concept from IT will only lead to short-lived gains at best (and is quite likely to extend the time needed for a business team to accept a new operating model).

OOOps at Cox Automotive

- Create **optionality** by unlocking core business capabilities via API-enabled digital services.
- Business and IT jointly identify **opportunities** by enabling innovations and market learnings to be shared across multiple lines of business.
- Drive **optimization** and continuous improvement through positioning API product teams as close as possible to revenue owners.

To create the conditions where the potential for uncapped benefits is maximized, organizations must strive to:

- Embrace the OOOps methods.
- Make the commitment to drive organizational design along the lines of multidisciplinary fusion teams that are positioned close to the point of revenue.
- Require delivery teams to take a product mindset in creating composable building blocks of small, self-describing chunks of interoperable value delivery.

Platform Maturity Follows Financial Maturity at Lowe's

Cox is not alone in its ability to transition smoothly between business eras, nor in its finance-grounded approach to leverage unbundling and APIs to thrive in the digital age. Another example comes from retail IT leader Steve Stone. Over his career, Stone developed and applied an approach to transformation focused on customer centricity, business-IT collaboration, near-term financial gains, and setting up feedback mechanisms to continually guide and adjust the course of his agenda.

Stone has always been a person who turns ideas into action. Early in his career, he recognized the importance of taking a modular approach to software systems to balance the contention between the optimization of their components versus the optimization of the cohesive whole. As a programmer, he favored modularization and encapsulation. "Laziness is a great motivator," he reflects. "I didn't want to code edits twice."[18] He has used this insight in his many roles since.

At the start of his career, Stone gained broad experience in IT, first as a project manager for Management Science America and then as an IT consultant at Ernst & Young. He brought this experience to home improvement retailer Lowe's in 1992. Working his way up through the IT organization, he became CIO in 2003.

As the overall leader of IT, Stone focused on how the line of business teams worked with IT. He found that IT tended to work in isolation from the business. Requirements for business initiatives would be sent to IT, which would then provide estimates back to a business-technology steering committee for prioritization and funding. IT would then work on the funded initiatives while the business teams went back to their day jobs.

According to Stone, business teams would often overstuff their initiative requests to maximize their impact. "They never knew when they were going to get IT again, so they would have everything and the kitchen sink thrown in," he recollects. "As a result, a typical program at Lowe's—a three to four project program—would take around twenty-six months to deliver. One that I remember took six years and $1.4 billion with little impact."[19]

He recognized that it would be difficult to stay current with the industry when working on such long cycle times, and he was concerned about the business impact IT could have in this setting. Still, Stone felt that from the CIO seat, he might be in one of the best positions to have a big impact on the Lowe's business strategy.

Following a discussion with a third-party consultant on Lowe's channel integration needs, Stone remarked that it wasn't channel integration they needed; it was channel obliteration. The name stuck and Stone went about writing up a channel obliteration white paper to define a strategy for how Lowe's could remove barriers between its customers and the value it provided to them. He notes, "The idea of channel obliteration was really to put the customer at the front of the experience."[20]

In Stone's vision, Lowe's customers could start their journey at any point of interaction—online, in-store, or on the phone—and progress that journey using the appropriate channels at the right time without disruption. To illustrate the vision, Stone focused on one of the harder home improvement projects: kitchen renovations.

"In kitchens you have appliances, you have rough plumbing, fashion plumbing, lighting, tiles," he outlines. "All of these are different products that can be ordered from different manufacturers and put in by different installers."[21]

The vision was compelling, but the business-IT communication challenges meant it took a couple of years to take hold within Lowe's.

Eventually, the business did get on board and effectively adopted channel obliteration as the mantra for the Lowe's business vision. To support the reimagining of their customer journeys, they built an "experience lab" at headquarters. This was a facility that allowed them to simulate the buyer's journey at all phases.

"Through that lab, we learned interesting details," recalls Stone. "For example, we found that the average flooring customer would visit the store six times before making their flooring purchase. This allowed us to examine when they were making their decisions, and how we could improve the process to accelerate that decision."[22]

They were able to take insights derived from the lab and address them through new capabilities. In one case, they identified a bottleneck in their handling of special orders, one that required special handling, which led to a long and laborious process. Lowe's succeeded in speeding up the customer experience but ended up overwhelming the invoice department, which now had to deal with a flood of one-off orders. Through examples like these, Stone noticed the contention between optimizing one part of the digital landscape and its consequential effect on other areas.

During his time at Lowe's, Stone had a big impact, and he saw the organization evolve in a positive direction. The company had grown from being a $3.5 billion company when he joined to $50 billion when he left in 2011. Business and IT collaboration had improved, especially through the experience lab, but IT was still working in relative isolation when it came time to execute new initiatives. Stone's assessment is that "part of that was the operating model, part of it was the business wanting IT resources dedicated to specific business areas and projects."[23]

He sees an opportunity for IT organizations within companies like Lowe's to put more focus on business impact rather than pure technology initiatives: "Channel obliteration was an example where I was trying to drive more revenue for the business, but that was more the exception than the rule."[24]

After driving change at Lowe's for nearly two decades, Stone recognized it was time for a change of his own and went on to apply his learnings first as

CIO of L Brands (operator of Victoria's Secret, Bath & Body Works, and others) and more recently with his own consulting business to provide guidance to leading companies in retail technology.

When the COVID-19 pandemic hit, Stone saw a major change in the way retailers were addressing their digital needs. "Companies were having to come up with new business models quickly because they didn't have the luxury of time," he states. "Business teams had to work hand in hand with IT because the requirements were so fluid."[25]

He believes this new operating model, where there is more collaboration between lines of business and IT teams, will set these companies up for success in the digital economy and avoid some of the pitfalls he experienced at Lowe's and L Brands.

Still, the rush to digitally transform overnight in response to the pandemic has left some residue for these retailers. "There's a lot of rework going on now because the solutions were not architecturally sound," says Stone.[26] He believes these companies shouldn't assume they have to throw everything away. In fact, it was this mindset shift to use their existing assets that helped get retailers through the pandemic.

"Instead of thinking 'How do I replace or remove technology?' leaders should think about innovative ways to reuse it," Stone advises. "One of the things that came out of the pandemic was retailers realizing they needed to reuse what they had, since they didn't have time to bring in all new stuff."[27]

He sees the composable approach he adopted at L Brands as the enabler that allows companies to "assemble things to solve problems as opposed to building it all from scratch."[28] Companies that embraced this approach before the pandemic have fared well. In Stone's words, "These people who were further along on this notion of composability are really weathering the storm much, much better than the ones who aren't."[29] With unknown future storms coming, he believes this is the best way to prepare.

In both the Lowe's and L Brands context, the OOOps methods took the path of gentle pressure relentlessly applied to digitize and optimize their physical business models. This conviction and willingness to bring business and finance stakeholders along the journey paid off both in financial terms and in changing the posture of business teams toward transformation topics.

OOOps at Lowe's

- Create **optionality** and enable consumers to seamlessly move between channels via API-enabled digital services.
- Business and IT jointly identify **opportunities** by enabling a realistic "experience lab" to simulate the buyer's journey at all phases.
- Drive **optimization** and continuous improvement through monitoring and experimenting within key revenue-producing customer journeys.

Closing the Chasm

Exchange optimization delivers more than just financial gain. This strategy requires both technology and business teams to challenge themselves. Both teams must achieve a deeper understanding and collaboration than many organizations are used to. But it is this collaboration—focused on delivering results grounded in financial and operational realities—that can help an organization overcome the historical divide between business and technology teams. In our next chapter, we'll uplevel our conversation and dive into the world of distributed innovation.

Strategies of Success #2: Distributed Innovation

We've just seen how the OOOps methods have been applied strategically to help organizations optimize value exchanges in their existing business models. In this chapter, we explore the distributed innovation digital success strategy. This pattern shows how organizations are engaging the widest possible community of digital builders using the OOOps methods— unbundled business capabilities, value dynamics, and feedback loops—and using that community to drive new products, services, and business models. We will look at how some of the most successful API product companies have leveraged external developer communities. We'll examine in detail how Coca-Cola has benefited from empowering its customers and how Anderson Holdings has benefited from empowering its non-IT employees.

Digital Demand Exceeds Builder Supply

One of the challenges every organization faces in the digital economy is trying to find more people to do the work. As we have illustrated, there are all sorts of opportunities for practical innovation in digital business. However, the standard practices of even the savviest digital companies have required skilled software developers to exploit these opportunities. Developer productivity—one of the tenets of the DevOps movement—has been a massive focus of the technology industry in the last several years, but the fact remains that there will always be an upper limit on the number of skilled developers in the general population.

In 2022, leading market intelligence firm IDC estimated there were around sixteen million developers globally,[1] compared to over a billion knowledge workers[2]—people who are users of information technology in their daily jobs. It stands to reason that the productivity gain of empowering these knowledge workers to be builders of digital solutions would be greater than the impact of further optimizing developers' work. So, a big way an organization could boost its digital production would be to involve its non-IT knowledge workers in the development of digital products and services. But this is not the only way.

Digital technologies allow organizations to be more interconnected. Another way to overcome software developer scarcity is to benefit your business through the work of developers who don't work for you. By allowing external developers to use tools that align with their goals and propel your own, you can significantly reduce the time, cost, and risk of digital experimentation. Depending on the business context, these developers could be self-employed entrepreneurs, weekend hobbyists, or members of the IT organization in a large partner company. The bottom line is, with the right incentives and tools, these external developers can create many new digital options for your business without excessive cost and coordination.

A final way digital production can be distributed beyond traditional IT delivery is by leveraging the consumption of digital products and services. In other words, companies can have their own customers become sources of business innovation. As with the other two approaches, the key to making this work is providing the right tools and incentives for customers to provide their input while benefiting themselves. This is made feasible by digital delivery and instrumentation.

All three of these new sources of distributed innovation—internal knowledge workers, external developers, and end customers—can be opened by applying the science of happy accidents. Unbundling business capabilities into API-enabled digital building blocks creates the foundation for the tools that each of these groups can use to drive innovation. Value dynamics provides a method for balancing incentives and creating "win-win" scenarios between an organization and its stakeholders. Feedback loops provide the means for collecting the innovation inputs. This is not just theory. It has been proven through several experiences. Let's look at some specific examples that illustrate each of these opportunities.

An API Economy

Earlier, we told the story of Tim O'Reilly evangelizing the value of APIs to Jeff Bezos in 2002. It is notable that at that time, O'Reilly specifically cited the potential for distributed innovation. In O'Reilly's words, "Giving developers a playground extends your development staff, bringing in new ideas and features at the same time as it builds your brand and image."[3] O'Reilly's prediction came true.

It may have been eBay that got O'Reilly so excited about APIs in the first place. The online auction site launched its first open APIs in 2000,[4] aiming to have its services embedded in the explosion of websites being launched at the time. The strategy paid off. eBay's API was used by some website developers to list their products for sale on eBay's site, and it was used by others to sell eBay-brokered products on theirs. Without the API, eBay would have needed to provide infrastructure for developers to build their complete sites on the eBay platform, a higher-risk, higher-cost proposition. Through APIs, eBay was able to support many more business model permutations and a broader community of developers.

As discussed earlier, the Google Maps public API was created as a response to developers reverse engineering Google's private API for its Maps web application. Just as with eBay, developers were able to embed Google's mapping services into their applications in novel ways that were not possible using the original Google Maps app.

Amazon Web Services CEO Adam Selipsky has talked about the "developer hunger" he observed when AWS's APIs were first launched in 2002.[5] This interest motivated the investment that led to AWS's reinvention in 2006 into a web development platform. From there, AWS's product strategy has frequently incorporated the innovations of its developer customers.

By opening its platform to third-party developers, Facebook similarly distributed its innovation. As Steve Yegge noted in his famous online rant, "Facebook is successful because they built an entire constellation of products by allowing other people to do the work."[6] These digital pirates all benefited from the distributed innovation pattern by unbundling their services through APIs.

In fact, this business model of using APIs to reach developers as customers created its own economy. The rise of mobile devices, social networks, and cloud computing provided new opportunities and greater productivity for developers. The urgency of capitalizing on these opportunities combined with the web's accessibility created a whole new economy of APIs.

As demonstrated in the rideshare example presented earlier in the book, services like Google Maps and AWS were used as building blocks for successful, developer-driven mobile startups. So were second-generation web unicorns like Twilio (whose APIs are used to support communication services like telephony, messaging, and billing) and Stripe (whose APIs are used for payments). The "API economy" defined by these pirates has continued to grow. Today, there are commercially available APIs covering innumerable industries and geographic regions. For example, banking aggregation services in North America are available through Plaid, while startup Okra provides similar services for the burgeoning digital startup scene in Nigeria. Unbundled, API-enabled digital services have proven to be developer-friendly, stand-alone products.

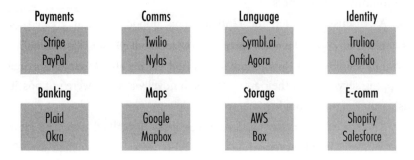

FIGURE 7.1: API Economy Categories with Notable Constituents

However, providing a platform—or elements of a platform—to developers is not the only way to distribute innovation for your business. Furthermore, digital pirates are not the only ones taking advantage of distributed innovation. Some of the most intriguing ways of driving productivity and ingenuity from a wider group of people come from long-established companies that have used some fresh thinking.

Coca-Cola's Secret Formula for Innovation

Earlier, we told the story of the experiment that led to Coca-Cola becoming a happy accident. The spirit of experimentation lives on at the Coca-Cola Company, right through to its digital presence today.

Coca-Cola Enterprises recognized the potential for digital transformation relatively early. Between 2006 and 2008, the company focused its IT efforts on solidifying operations, driving efficiencies, and saving costs. That same window of time saw the introduction of cloud computing with AWS, the launch of the mobile revolution with Apple's iPhone and App Store, and the start of the big data movement through the popularization of Hadoop. These industry innovations presented new opportunities for enterprises like Coca-Cola.

Notably, Coke's business and IT organizations assessed these technological opportunities jointly. In the past, business leaders may have formulated the company's strategy on their own and then handed the project list to IT. In this case, IT's success in driving operational efficiencies got Coca-Cola's CIO at the time, Esat Sezer, a seat at the strategy table. "That paid dividends to Coca-Cola Enterprises so significantly that it changed the perception of IT," he recalls. "We went from being viewed as a barrier to what the business wanted to do digitally to a partner they could team up with and move forward with together."[7] Once he had a seat at the table, Sezer made sure he made the most of the opportunity.

In organizations where there is a big divide between business teams and IT, technology changes are often implemented under the banner of "legacy modernization," without a lot of thought toward how they might impact the business. With business and IT leaders at the same table, Coca-Cola Enterprises considered how it could leverage these new digital options to modernize Coke's business rather than just its technology landscape. The company started by thinking through functional modernization. This involved identifying key business functions across all business lines: commercial, supply chain, and back office. Many of these core functions resided in legacy applications that ran on-premises. Coca-Cola's approach was to move these to best-of-breed SaaS providers. This functional modernization increased Coca-Cola's agility, reduced its overall operating costs, and simplified its accounting.

To enable this functional modernization, Sezer also had to deliver infrastructure modernization. The Coca-Cola team found they could not migrate to the new SaaS applications without changing their architectural approach to integration. Up to this point, many of Coca-Cola's applications were connected through opaque, point-to-point integrations that could not be reused. Using the business's platform mindset, Coca-Cola's IT teams used APIs to encapsulate the application functions and then layered them according to how they were being consumed. This API-based approach provided a level of insulation between user-facing applications and back-end systems that made it easier to migrate to the new SaaS solutions.

The approach of unbundling business capabilities through APIs also helped address an impedance mismatch in the organization (where friction and conflict arise between teams within an enterprise due to differences in how each team can manage the speed of change). As Coca-Cola embraced Agile approaches to developing their user-facing applications—moving to rapid iterations of software delivery—they found they were bottlenecked on their backend dependencies, systems that only changed three times per year. By fronting the backend systems with APIs, they were able to accommodate the required speed of delivery and decrease their time to value.

The dialogue was now open and healthy between business and IT leaders. Sezer was able to demonstrate to the business that by delivering these modernized capabilities as shared services across the organization, the business would be able to achieve the productivity gains they were seeking. "Any leader in a big corporation, as much as they are driven by growth, they are also driven by productivity," Sezer points out. "Through these successes, the modernization program was able to maintain momentum, and it became a foundation for Coca-Cola's digital transformation."[8] As Coke's digital transformation progressed, the strategy team adopted the mindset that they were turning the enterprise into a platform of business capabilities or—in their terms—creating a digital ecosystem.

Sezer sees digital ecosystems as the place "where the real business value is created."[9] Coca-Cola's ecosystem strategy featured some key tenets. First, they productize business capabilities through APIs. Although Coke's leadership assumed those APIs might be reused beyond their original purpose, they didn't over-engineer the APIs with unknown consumers in mind. Second, Coca-Cola consciously expanded the scope of their ecosystem strategy from the core outward—from internal capabilities to suppliers and distributors to end consumers and ultimately to new products and services. Last, Coca-Cola put a big emphasis on implementing "sense and respond" mechanisms within their ecosystems, recognizing that feedback loops were essential to maximizing the value of digital business.

"We had great analytics and report generation, great project management discipline, a great software development life cycle, but that didn't help us figure out what consumers wanted and allow us to quickly deliver it," Sezer says. "Sense and respond discipline was the key to making that happen."[10] In effect, Coca-Cola Enterprises had implemented the three OOOps methods that define the science of happy accidents.

OOOps at Coca-Cola

- Create **optionality** by unbundling core business capabilities into API-enabled digital services.
- Business and IT jointly identify **opportunities** by aligning tech innovations with business needs.
- Drive **optimization** through "sense and respond" capabilities in the digital ecosystem.

The idea of optionality was a big part of Coke's philosophy. Solutions built into Coca-Cola's new digital ecosystem had two aspects: what they delivered and what they enabled. In addition to solving a near-term problem or exploiting a current business opportunity, each initiative also needed to create reusable pieces of the puzzle that could be leveraged for future value and innovation. Once Coca-Cola got good at delivering these API-enabled puzzle pieces, they had the confidence and courage to start mapping out the core domains of their business and become more experimental with technology. Two examples— image recognition and augmented reality—show how this paid off.

Coca-Cola first used image recognition technology to improve its shelf counting process (as we related earlier in the book). Moving from manual shelf counting to automated counting via image recognition brought huge productivity gains, as well as higher-fidelity data. The same image recognition tech was reused to reduce the cycle count process from a day to an hour, leading to more store availability and ultimately more revenue for their distributors. Exercising these options—leveraging the same digital capability in two different contexts—was possible due to the API enablement of the image recognition capability and the empowerment of different lines of business to use the new capability: innovation distributed.

Augmented reality (AR) was first deployed at Coca-Cola to help sell coolers to outlets. Rather than flip through printed catalogs or scroll through web pages, Coca-Cola's salespeople could use their phones to show store owners what the coolers would look like in their locations. This had a positive impact on close rates for sales. This AR tech was then reused to help field technicians identify needed parts for repairs. Rather than taking machines apart to identify replacement parts, they were able to use AR to "see into" the machines and identify the faulty parts more rapidly. This made the repair technicians more productive and saved repair costs.

Once again, the combination of unbundled capabilities and empowered business teams helped Coca-Cola find buried treasure. "We started to expand those composable components into different areas—services, sales, warehouses, wherever you want—that were never anticipated when first looking at these new technologies," Sezer explains. "Once they were made composable through APIs and teams could experiment with them, they found the right applications and looked for more ways to use them."[11] A final example shows how Coca-Cola's adoption of the OOOps methods revolutionized its digital business.

Consumer-Driven R&D with Freestyle Fountains

One of the big challenges facing consumer goods companies is how to create direct relationships with their consumers. In the analog business world, customer relationship management is mostly handled by retailers that sell packaged goods. In that paradigm, Coca-Cola built up a strong soda dispensary business at retail locations like fast food restaurants and movie theaters. The value exchange model for this business is shown in Figure 7.2.

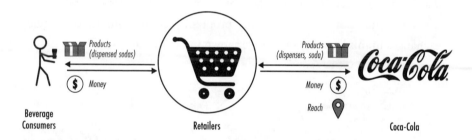

FIGURE 7.2: Business Model for Coca-Cola's Soda Dispensers in 2008

In 2009, Coca-Cola introduced its Freestyle soda fountains, which allowed consumers to customize their beverages. Consumers could select and combine to create new flavors, which was certainly a new value proposition for them. In addition, by connecting the Freestyle machines to the web, Coca-Cola was also able to create a channel for gathering data about beverage customization and consumption. This not only allowed improved operational efficiency but also informed Coca-Cola's product development plans. The post-Freestyle business model is shown in Figure 7.3.

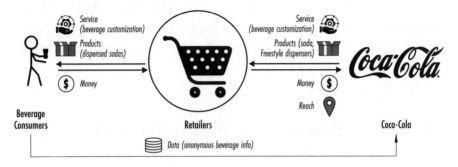

FIGURE 7.3: Business Model for Coca-Cola's Soda Dispensers in 2013

In 2018, Coca-Cola rolled out a new generation of Freestyle machines that allowed individual consumers to connect via Bluetooth and do things like customize and order drinks from apps on their smartphones. This provided an even better experience for consumers and enhanced the quality of data being collected by Coca-Cola, which could attribute data to individual users and incorporate it into loyalty programs, as an example. The value exchanges in this business model are shown in Figure 7.4.

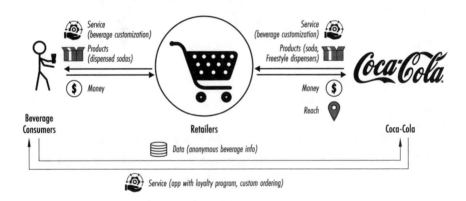

FIGURE 7.4: Business Model for Coca-Cola's Soda Dispensers in 2018

With this step, Coca-Cola effectively crowdsourced some of the research and development of their beverage flavors. They created a bidirectional channel for interaction with their consumers and had it tied to a service those consumers found valuable. Analyzing these value exchanges through value dynamics helps to illustrate the power of these innovations clearly.

Freestyle fountains help Coca-Cola Enterprises distribute its product innovation. Using the built-in, API-enabled "sense and respond" mechanisms in its ecosystem, Coca-Cola can conduct real-time market research through the Freestyle fountains. "Today you have orange-flavored Coke on the shelves as a result of these machines," says Sezer.[12] These win-win scenarios—where the consumer and service provider both benefit from a single innovation—are the hallmark of a high-functioning digital ecosystem, and APIs are the unbundling mechanism, the method of value exchange, and the conduits that create the digital feedback loop.

Reflecting on his time at Coca-Cola, Esat Sezer saw a huge amount of change in a relatively short time. "In twelve years, we came from a period where IT's role was being questioned to a point where we found ourselves in the middle of the business," he says. "I went from running a cost center to being a P&L owner."[13] It was the ecosystem approach that he felt was most impactful in that time. "Creating digital ecosystems was transformational," he states. "We were able to create novel value in those ecosystems, which is what digital transformation is all about."[14]

But he also gives a reminder of what made those ecosystems possible: "If you don't address legacy modernization in parallel with digital transformation, you won't be able to move with the speed and pace needed to drive value for the business."[15]

Coke's adoption of the OOOps methods—unbundling through APIs, identifying technology-enabled business opportunities, and optimizing through sense and response—was foundational to its success and allowed innovation to be distributed across all teams and even to its consumers.

Digital Transformation Takes Hold at Anderson Holdings

Let's turn now to an example that shows how even smaller companies with a long legacy can become digital pirates. Anderson Holdings may seem like an unlikely success story when it comes to digital transformation. The

California-based holding company's six subsidiaries cut across a variety of long-established industries—automotive, real estate, insurance, and beverages. Not what you might see as fertile ground when it comes to digital innovation. Then again, you would probably also call it unlikely for the teenage son of a barber from Minnesota who left home for UCLA to ultimately become a self-made billionaire with that university's school of management named after him. But that's exactly what happened to Anderson Holdings' founder, John E. Anderson, after he packed up his ice skates and headed southwest in 1936 on a hockey scholarship.[16]

The journey from those humble beginnings to Anderson's ultimate success is nothing like a straight line. He graduated Phi Beta Kappa from UCLA, earned an MBA from Harvard, enlisted in the Navy when the US entered World War II, passed his CPA while serving, obtained his law degree, and started a law firm by 1950. While teaching and practicing law, he began making investments in beverage distribution, real estate, and car dealerships. As his business empire grew, he and his wife expanded their philanthropy with donations to children's hospitals, community organizations, and his alma mater. Never a man to rest on his laurels, Anderson used every achievement in his life to open new possibilities for his next moves. Anderson's life is a remarkable one, and it serves as an analogy for the way Anderson Holdings and its subsidiaries have approached digital transformation.

Topa Insurance is one such subsidiary. After joining Topa in 2014, then CIO Brian Schween was tasked with migrating Topa's core insurance system to a new platform. Typically, a core migration like this would involve months of painstaking requirements work followed by vendor selection and the hiring of a solutions integrator to implement and integrate the new system. The result would often be a highly customized system that was costly and complicated to evolve.

Schween took a different approach, as we learned in our interview with him. First, he convinced his business partners to forgo the lengthy requirements process. He recalls telling them, "Let's use a best-of-breed system for six months and see what it's lacking. I promise we can make changes to meet the needs, but I want you to try it first. Otherwise, we're going to implement our same operating model on top of a brand-new insurance system and wreck it."[17] That move took the focus off trying to replicate the current system's functions and put the focus on what the business needed.

The second facet of his approach was to apply a capability lens, not just zeroing in on the functional scope provided by the vendor solutions. After analyzing the full set of capabilities in the environment, he and his team prioritized the ones they knew would require the most rapid and frequent change—namely Rating and Forms. They knew they would require an architecture that would allow those capabilities to evolve dynamically.

That led to the third aspect of the approach, which was to first establish the integration approach for the IT landscape before focusing on the core system in the enterprise architecture. Schween's approach was to "get everything connected and talking, data flowing, and then think about how to drop in an ERP or core system into that type of environment."[18]

The core system migration and the emphasis on composable business capabilities paid off. "We could make changes in hours that took weeks in the systems we replaced," Schween notes. "Not only did we have this enterprise application integration layer and best-of-breed components, but the core system we bought was built on a componentized services framework."[19]

Aside from the accomplishment of just migrating the core system, the re-architecture of the IT landscape resulted in new levels of agility and velocity Topa's business leaders had not anticipated. Prior to migration, Topa was offering four products across six systems. After the migration, they were able to offer more than one hundred new state-product combinations created by one business analyst and a single developer. Schween states that the migration allowed his business partners to "expand their product mix, turn around revisions, and capitalize on new relationships at a speed that they didn't even ask for."[20] Topa had unbundled its core insurance capabilities using this new approach, and its business leaders started exercising their options.

Through his time at Topa, Schween had been briefing Anderson's board of directors quarterly on the state of technology. The chair was impressed and doubled down by inviting Schween to move up to the parent company to bring similar innovation at headquarters and across the Anderson subsidiaries. Schween's new title was chief digital officer for the parent company, a reflection of his innovation focus as well as a break from the cost center connotations of the CIO title. Schween brought on his longtime colleague Denny Pichardo as director of technology and innovations soon after.

When Schween and Pichardo arrived at Anderson headquarters, they found an IT green field. Employees had desktop support and some outsourced application support, but there were no software developers to be found. Instead of being alarmed by the lack of technical resources, they were encouraged. The unbundling approach Schween had succeeded with at Topa was built on Lean principles, and there would be no status quo to overcome at Anderson. They got to work applying the approach right away.

At a holding company, the core competency is financial management. Whereas customer-facing companies—including Anderson's subsidiaries—relegate their financial ledger-based activities to the back office, for Anderson this is the primary focus of the front office. At the outset, financial reporting and settlement were manual activities involving spreadsheets and arduous reconciliation.

A typical approach to optimizing these processes might have been to study the current state activities and codify them in a new application, but that's not how Schween and Pichardo went about it. Instead, they started by talking to Anderson's financial analysts to understand what was and wasn't working and where the biggest pain points were. This allowed them to uplevel the conversation and discover opportunities for improved business outcomes rather than entrenching suboptimal processes in new technology. Like Coca-Cola's approach, they focused their digital transformation efforts on modernizing the business processes, not just the underlying technology.

Through this approach, they found that the most impactful starting point was to improve the monthly close process for Anderson. At the end of every month, Anderson must reconcile account activity with all its subsidiaries. Prior to Schween and Pichardo joining, this process involved manual input, one-to-one conversations, and a lot of headaches. Schween and Pichardo wanted to streamline it and make it fun.

The first thing they did was open API access to the data sources at headquarters and the subsidiaries to make automation of the close process possible. "They didn't have access to 90% of their data when we landed and we just unlocked it," recalls Schween. "They were like, 'Oh my god, I didn't even know we had this data!'"[21] With the data now usable, Schween and Pichardo created software-based automation that allowed Anderson's financial analysts to execute the close process in one click. To top it off, they used the enterprise engagement platform Slack to optimize and gamify the experience. "We used emojis to get the users' attention," says Pichardo. "If the close failed, we would react with warning emojis, and we were able to articulate what went wrong and how the user could resolve it. If the process succeeded, we would display celebratory emojis."[22] The new process was a hit, with each user clicking the close button almost like a pirate digging for buried treasure who gets to hear a satisfying "thunk" as the shovel hits the intended target almost immediately.

The new approach was such a success, Anderson analysts were now clamoring for more and more digital capabilities. They had always thought of IT as a support organization, but now they could see how digital solutions could be built specifically for their needs. The APIs that unlocked the systems and data were used to add value across the organization. "We got the onboarding time for new companies down from one month to two days," says Pichardo.[23]

In another example that came from further collaboration with the Anderson financial team, Schween and Pichardo found out that a big pain point came from subsidiary companies opening accounts that headquarters wouldn't learn about until month's end. "The number one issue we had every month was that there were new accounts in the subsidiaries that weren't in the holding company ERP, because nobody notified headquarters of the new accounts," Pichardo relates. "In the old system, this would cause the process to fail, and teams could spend days trying to figure out where the discrepancies were."[24]

The good news was that because account services had been unlocked through APIs already when automating the monthly close, they were able to rapidly implement a solution to the new account issue. By interrogating the HQ and subsidiary account systems, they were able to proactively identify discrepancies and ensure things were resolved prior to month end. This shows the value of optionality, and Anderson's resulting value exchanges are depicted in Figure 7.5.

By unbundling Anderson Holdings' systems and data through APIs, and surfacing these capabilities to business users in Slack, Schween and Pichardo were doing more than solving discrete business problems. They were transforming the organization and its members' mindset when it came to the possibilities of technology. Digitizing kernels of business value opened the opportunity to create combinatorial business value, leading to a non-linear increase in innovation opportunity.

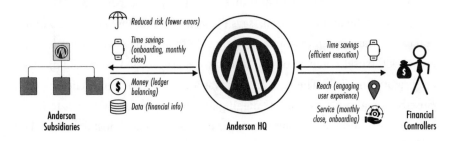

FIGURE 7.5: Value Exchanges as a Result of Anderson's Unbundling

"We start spinning up all these little things," says Pichardo. "Then we connect this thing to that thing, and we get this new value that we didn't anticipate at the beginning."[25] Even better, users felt empowered. "Those business users didn't have a partner in digital who could push the envelope before," states Pichardo. "Fast forward to today, and now they're thinking digitally. They're thinking about workflows they can enable and automate. They're pushing us harder now. They're saying, 'Why can't you automate this part? We don't want to do it manually.'"[26] Empowering these energized business partners to innovate helped accelerate Anderson's digital transformation. Anderson's approach aligns with the OOOps methods.

OOOps at Anderson Holdings

- Create **optionality** by unlocking data assets and creating APIs for core financial services.
- Business users identify **opportunities** by matching process improvements with available APIs.
- Drive **optimization** and continuous improvement through incentivized user experience.

In addition to unbundling, Schween and Pichardo included several key principles in their approach. For Schween, starting with a clean slate at Anderson Holdings allowed him to position the role of his organization differently than a typical IT organization. "I looked at this like a petri dish for a software company," says Schween. "When you've got to support a bunch of different companies across a wide range of industries and they're a captive audience, it's like building a startup from scratch."[27] Like a successful startup, Schween and Pichardo adopted Lean and Agile principles and have created a highly collaborative culture with their business partners. They have instituted fast feedback to ensure that anything they learn through experimentation and communication can be used to adjust course and open new opportunities.

Schween and Pichardo both argue that new opportunities can only be discovered through experimentation and taking intermediate steps. Schween feels the solutions they have implemented "exceed anything we would have gotten as requirements from a business user."[28] Pichardo goes a step further. "You're never going to get the exact requirements to innovate," he says. "That just doesn't happen. To innovate, people have to work together, see and feel something tangible, then iterate on that."[29]

Schween and Pichardo characterize what they're doing as a "platform approach." They see the collection of unbundled business capabilities and the underlying technologies that enable them as a platform for business innovation. The platform concept has resonated with their business partners, especially after their successes in automating away some of Anderson's biggest financial process pain points. To make the platform approach work, they have had to adjust the Lean concept of *minimum viable product* to *minimum viable extensible product*.

Pichardo explains, "As an architect, there is always a balancing act. Am I building something robust that can handle the needs of all these companies? Or am I doing something like a POC to show value quickly to this company? It's hard to provide value quickly while building something robust. The only way to do that is by using a composable approach."[30]

In its study of high-performing technology organizations, the book *Accelerate* states that a foundational capability of such organizations is "loosely coupled architecture."[31] Loose coupling in software architecture is about having a high-level agreement between components while allowing for flexibility in the details of how those components connect and communicate.

The way Schween and Pichardo have unbundled data and applications through APIs at Anderson Holdings promotes loose coupling in this sense. However, Schween and Pichardo apply this notion of loose coupling in all aspects of their platform approach. By focusing on business innovation through technology without a set of constraining plan-based steps, they have created a loosely coupled learning organization. Also, by focusing their collaboration with business teams on business problems rather than technical details, they have created a loosely coupled requirements gathering methodology. Loose coupling of the people, processes, and technology at Anderson has reduced unnecessary coordination across team boundaries, promoted actionable learning, and left room for the happy accidents that can lead to the most significant unanticipated innovations.

Calling All Pirates

There is a scarcity of skilled software engineers in the industry. The demand for digital solutions is vastly outpacing that developer supply. Adopting the OOOps methods of the science of happy accidents allows organizations to find new sources of distributed digital innovation and helps them scale their digital work. Public API pioneers like eBay and Amazon used APIs to engage developers in mutually beneficial work. This paved the way for a whole industry of API product companies, like Twilio and Stripe. Business and technology leaders at Coca-Cola teamed up using the unbundling approach to find practical uses for new technologies and introduced the Freestyle fountain to engage their customers in driving product innovation. Anderson Holdings combined unbundled business capabilities with the energy of its business users to optimize its business processes and accelerate time to value. Through the OOOps methods, innovation can be distributed inside and outside an enterprise.

8

Strategies of Success #3: Capability Capitalization

In this chapter, we round the corner and dive deep into what can be among the most lucrative digital success strategy: *capability capitalization*. This strategy focuses on how organizations leverage all three of the OOOps methods—unbundled business capabilities, value dynamics, and feedback loops—to unbundle and rebundle capabilities buried within their business. By doing so, they can create new products, services, and even highly profitable operating units that may test the limits of their brand elasticity. (Brand elasticity is defined as how far a company can stretch its brand to become a trusted seller of products and services that consumers don't already associate with it.) We will look at several examples of well-known enterprises that chose to take on new markets and, in a few cases, even create new market categories in which they could leverage first mover advantage to reap a windfall.

It's one thing to win in business. It's another thing to win big. It's a completely different thing to achieve a 10X win. The 10Xs are game-changing wins. Often in business, there is an element of luck in capturing wins of any size, like the happy accidents we've explored. This is even truer in the game-changing category. Thus, you might ask yourself, "What can I do about luck?" In his book *Great by Choice*, Jim Collins posits that luck isn't the defining factor for companies that over-achieve. Instead, he points to "return on luck."[1]

We're all hit in life with different kinds of luck. But a huge swing variable is there are those who grab it and then get a high return on that luck, and there are those who fritter it away. When you compound that over time, it tends to produce a very big difference.

The 10X cases and the comparisons both got luck, good and bad, in comparable amounts. The evidence leads us to conclude that luck does not cause 10X success. People do. The critical question is not "Are you lucky?" but "Do you get a high return on luck?"[2]

Less Is More Because Less Leaves Room for More

While luck may be evenly distributed and out of your control, the skills and capabilities to exploit that luck and make a return on it are in your control. Return on luck, good or bad, can often be optimized by creating, conserving, and exploiting optionality. The pattern of seemingly stumbling into big opportunities is well understood by the pre-digital business world, but inside the digital pirate community, a new methodology for seeking out and capturing the 10X wins has formed, grounded in API-based optionality, value dynamics, and an obsession with feedback loops.

This new methodology took shape with clear influences from the work of a Harvard professor who is widely regarded as one of the most influential management thinkers of our time—Clayton Christensen. Christensen, praised by industry leaders worldwide, including Jeff Bezos and Steve Jobs, illuminated the path to disruptive innovation and drove digital enterprises around the world to embrace modularity as a competitive asset.

These enterprises leverage all three of the OOOps methods to not only produce value for consumers but also create the specific tools they need to rapidly vet and exploit opportunities. AWS is the prime example of internally unbundled capabilities. Communications startup Twilio and payments company Stripe followed the path of Google Maps, unbundling widely needed industry capabilities and riding the mobile app boom to rapid growth. Aggregators like Uber and Airbnb bootstrapped their businesses on APIs from Twilio, Stripe, Google Maps, and AWS to rapidly disrupt the transportation and hospitality industries. As Tim O'Reilly had predicted, this collective innovation created a tide that raised all digital boats by allowing enterprises to become more productive not just in times of digital disruption but, perhaps, because of it by allowing enterprises to buy commodities (resource-intensive infrastructure) and build differentiation (products and experiences).

Amazon's Journey to Transform Muck into Money

Amazon was one of the early web success stories, quickly expanding their e-commerce product offerings beyond books to become a general retailer. Amazon was a pioneer in using the interactive nature of the web to collect customer feedback and observe customer behavior and then use it to customize the user experience. Figure 8.1 shows what the Amazon business model looked like around the turn of the millennium.

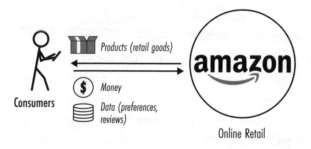

FIGURE 8.1: Business Model for Amazon in 2000

As discussed previously, Amazon made a conscious shift to unbundle its business capabilities through APIs around 2002. They used this approach to provide more scalable infrastructure that they needed to support the growth of their retail business. At the same time, they also launched public APIs to provide product catalog information to third-party developers. Those developers could build apps that would allow their users to shop for products that would be purchased and fulfilled through Amazon, thus expanding Amazon's reach. Amazon would in turn pay the developers' referral fees for such purchases. The resulting business model is shown in Figure 8.2.

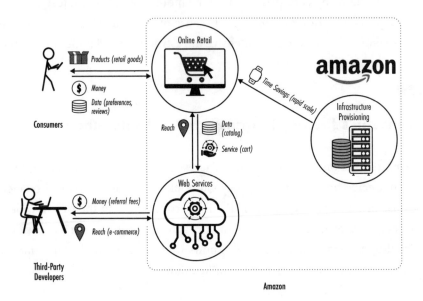

FIGURE 8.2: Business Model for Amazon in 2003

Using the value dynamics perspective, the eventual launch of Amazon Web Services as the web's first infrastructure-as-a-service business is easily foreseen. Amazon had built the infrastructure provisioning (setting up scaled data centers and making them secure, connected, and accessible with simple self-service web tools) capabilities to support its retail business. Amazon had also established a developer channel through its original retail-oriented collection of web services. All that was required was packaging those infrastructure provisioning services through the existing channel and appealing to their existing audience. Amazon did this in 2006 with the launch of its S3 and ECS services. The current business model is depicted in Figure 8.3.

This is a big example of how Amazon's unbundling approach paid dividends, but there are many more. Alexa, Kindle, Amazon Ads, and many other innovations were enabled and accelerated by piggybacking on capabilities that had been put in place initially for other purposes. Being able to leverage the OOOps methods and match digital capabilities with channels is unquestionably a key ingredient in Amazon's continued success.

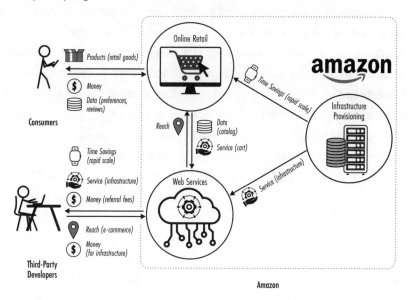

FIGURE 8.3: Business Model for Amazon in 2006

OOOps at Amazon

- Create **optionality** by unbundling core infrastructure capabilities into API-enabled digital services.
- Business leaders identify **opportunities** by aligning tech innovations with the global need for managed infrastructure services.
- Drive **optimization** and continuous improvement through institutionalizing "sense and respond" across every team and activity.

While this "shift to the cloud" has been highly visible for almost all enterprises over the last decade, we can trace its origins back to a talk given by Jeff

Bezos at MIT Tech Review's Emerging Technologies Conference in September of 2006. Entitled "We Build Muck, So You Don't Have To," Bezos laid out the problem that enterprises faced trying to bring products to market. The Amazon leadership had spotted an opportunity where startups and scaled enterprises all around the world were struggling with the time and resources necessary to do "the undifferentiated yet all-important 'heavy lifting' needed to create and operate a web application" including "server hosting, bandwidth management, contract negotiation, scaling and managing physical growth, dealing with the accumulated complexity of heterogeneous hardware, and coordinating the large teams needed to take care of each of these areas."[3]

In the years preceding this serendipitous moment, Amazon had become strikingly adept at each one of these capabilities, stating, "After being in business for nearly eleven years, we know how to make great muck at Amazon!"[4] Even more striking than the strength of Amazon's capabilities was the fact that Amazon had been building toward this moment since 2002 when Bezos had issued the API mandate (spoken to in detail in Chapter 1). Amazon not only had a great set of digital capabilities, but it also ensured these decontextualized capabilities could be leveraged by external users without having to redesign and rebuild them for a new range of use cases.

With the amazing success of AWS, the idea of leveraging services that others can do faster, better, and cheaper than you has become a foundational concept for successfully transforming business and operating models. When looking at the frequent build-versus-buy decisions that come your way, this doesn't necessarily mean *always buy*. The posture to embrace within your transformation efforts can be explained with two different ideas:

1. First, shift the default build-versus-buy position to buy as the default and build as the exception, which must have a solid business case for the use of financial resources.
2. If in the process of examining the build-versus-buy question in a particular problem space, you find the buy options significantly limited or onerous to integrate into your enterprise, consider whether there might be an opportunity for a market-facing service that your enterprise could capitalize on.

While it might be tempting for digital pirates and settlers to think that the boom times of Amazon creating AWS have depleted the inventory of possible 10X wins, we urge you to look at the last two decades as the beginning of an optionality-driven economy built upon a digital island filled with unknown treasure waiting to be discovered via a series of happy accidents. One must only look at the parade of organizations that have unearthed their own accidental treasures (and perhaps those organizations that passed them by as well). Creating useful APIs to drive more optionality for individual companies (regardless of industry or size) has become part of the digital success playbook, specifically because the web has become a scaled playground for happy accidents.

Slack: Lessons Are Learned More by People Than by the Institutions That Employ Them

One such happy accident started as a video game company before becoming the fastest-growing B2B startup in history: Slack. We touched on Slack's origin story earlier in this book. Now, we're going to take a deeper dive.

Slack's origin story should not come as a surprise, given that its founder, Stewart Butterfield, did almost the exact same thing at his previous company, Flickr. Like Slack, Flickr also started as a game company that chose to pivot and focus on one small aspect (i.e., photo sharing). Also, like Slack, Flickr was passionate about the feedback-driven iteration of their offering. So much so that Flickr's devotion to lowering their cost to experiment is credited as one of the pivotal moments that caused the DevOps movement to go viral when John Allspaw and Paul Hammond shared their love for speed at the 2009 Velocity Conference with the viral talk "10+ Deploys Per Day at Flickr."

After selling Flickr to Yahoo! in 2005, founder Stewart Butterfield left Yahoo! in 2008 and soon after started yet another game company called Tiny Speck. While Tiny Speck had some modest success with the multiplayer online game *Glitch*, Butterfield soon recognized that the collaboration capabilities offered within the game had singular potential. In a classic case of unbundling, Tiny Speck morphed into a new company, Slack, and took aim at an entirely new class of customers with its new stand-alone collaboration product.

With an ambition to replace email at companies of all sizes, Slack experienced meteoric growth in its early days due to the amazing combination of its sticky UI for chat paired (perhaps more importantly) with its no-code ecosystem approach powered by APIs. Slack's differentiating rocket fuel over other collaboration tools was its out-of-the-box integration with third-party services like Dropbox, Twitter, and Zendesk. APIs provided by these companies were the mechanism to make this possible, and the team at Slack recognized the potential of giving their users APIs to build their own customizations and automations.

During our research for this book, we had the good fortune to be able to speak with an engineering veteran who crossed paths with Butterfield at both Yahoo! and Slack: Saurabh Sahni. Sahni, currently a principal software engineer at Slack, has always been passionate about connecting people, especially developers, and empowering them to build new things in new ways. Sahni is an expert in the craft of platform building—that is, building tools that other people use to build their own products, solutions, and automations.

When Sahni joined Yahoo! in 2007, it was a haven of technological innovation. The Apache Hadoop open-source project that spawned the big data revolution had roots at Yahoo! in this period.[5] Yahoo! was also an early adopter of web APIs both externally and internally, using them to drive innovation in its ecosystem.[6] Sahni was blown away by the wealth of APIs at his disposal, which could be used to build new products and services easily: "We had APIs for everything: weather, finance, stocks, search, ads."[7] This landscape was a developer's dream.

However, as Sahni became more acquainted with Yahoo!'s business, he noticed an interesting phenomenon. Although many of these APIs were popular with developers, that didn't always translate into business success for the company. There were some that worked well, like their ads API, thanks to Apple's policy that ensured Yahoo! got paid for ads presented in iPhone apps. Conversely, some APIs were damaging to Yahoo!'s business model. By allowing Yahoo!'s data to be accessed by customers on other companies' web properties—such as a stock quoting app using Yahoo!'s finance API—Yahoo!

was missing potential traffic on its own web properties. There was a misalignment between the healthy environment of technological innovation and the business model itself.

Sahni (who joined Slack in 2015) was immediately intrigued by Slack's platform vision and the potential for building APIs within an organization that had attained product and engineering alignment. "Slack is a product-driven company," he states. "Engineering is focused on enabling the goals of the core business, and the APIs we build follow suit."[8] Product teams work closely with business development partners and directly with customers to understand their needs. Sahni's platform group works closely with the development community to ensure their feedback drives the API strategy.

When Sahni joined Slack, he started right away on applying his learnings from Yahoo! to the Slack platform. He noticed that the Slack engineering team was writing a lot of code to make those third-party integrations work. This was necessary to create a draw for customers to use Slack, but the approach would be difficult to scale. "We called it a platform, but at that time it wasn't," Sahni says.[9] The team found that when third-party providers made breaking changes to their APIs, the engineering team could be caught off guard and need to scramble to resolve issues. It wasn't a sustainable situation.

To truly make Slack a platform, Sahni believed they would need the right APIs so partners could do the work to create their own integrations, and the time was right. Slack's popularity with users created the right incentive for partners to do just that. "The evolution from product to platform is all about letting users build," Sahni says. "We are enabling customers to build the automations they want."[10] Slack did this by unbundling its product capabilities through APIs, providing developer-friendly services to make it easy to use those APIs, and creating an app directory where partners could offer their API-enabled solutions.

This platform approach opened the floodgates for Slack, helping to overcome the prior scaling bottlenecks. As of this writing, there are over 2,400 apps and bots in the Slack directory.[11] The app developers range from tech giants like Google and Microsoft to individual developers publishing apps that provide "dad jokes" and "cat facts." The cost to Slack only kicks in as apps are used, and it scales with their popularity. This is a three-party model that works harmoniously: app providers get access to a growing user base, users get access to more services, and Slack's overall business grows. "When we were so small, if we had just opened up APIs, none of these partners would have built integrations with Slack," says Sahni. "Once we had momentum, it was much easier to attract these partners and have them own their apps and integrations using our APIs."[12]

Partners and app developers are not the only users of Slack's APIs. Slack's customers can also use Slack's APIs to automate processes, and there are even some APIs purpose-built for Slack admins at big organizations. Slack's API consumer base continues to grow. "We have a million developers using our APIs today," notes Sahni. "Even so, how can we tell if these are long-tail developers or truly the developers we need to drive our business?"[13] This continuous focus on aligning the consumption of Slack's services—which drive its operational costs—with the value it captures is essential to scaling Slack's business model (Figures 8.4 and 8.5 illustrate how the Slack business model evolved to place a greater emphasis on third-party developers).

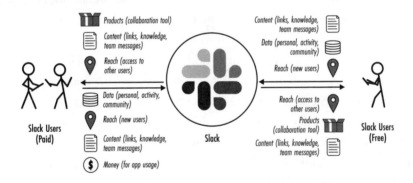

FIGURE 8.4: Slack's Original Value Exchange Model

Slack's organization has evolved as its business has scaled. Slack was a pioneer in having a dedicated customer experience (CX) team. At the time they launched their first APIs, it was just the CX and Engineering teams that brought the APIs to market and managed their life cycles. As Slack grew and matured, more teams were involved: Marketing, Business Development, Platform, Solutions Engineering, User Research, and Developer Relations.

Feedback loops are also a fundamental ingredient to Slack's success with its platform strategy. Many teams are involved in measuring the effectiveness of APIs at each stage of their life cycle. At the earliest stage, Product Design and Engineering publish the APIs. Business Development builds new partnerships based on the APIs. Developer Marketing and Customer Marketing share what is being built with partners and end users respectively. Technical Architects and User Research work with customers to get feedback. Developer Relations and Partner Engineering work with customers on an ongoing basis, with DevRel maintaining a particular focus on long-tail developers—those developers who don't fit the profile of Slack's target customers—to identify new opportunities. Slack is not only using these APIs as a means of delivering value but also as a data collection source to measure that value and to find new value channels.

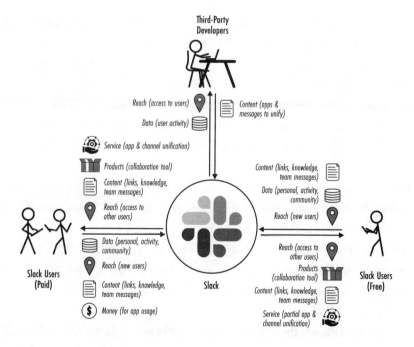

FIGURE 8.5: Slack's Evolved Value Exchange Model with a Greater Emphasis on Third-Party Partners

Sahni believes this continual examination of API consumption is essential. "One of the reasons market research is so critical is that we have a million developers using Slack APIs," he says. "Every developer that joins the wagon is helping make Slack better."[14] He believes strongly that companies shouldn't just launch APIs for APIs' sake. "For companies, is the API a checkbox to show they have one, or is the API really something that will grow your business? If it's not in the second category, every investment should be questioned."[15] This scrutiny is institutionalized at Slack.

Looking at both the present and the future, Sahni sees the platform model working very well. "Slack is heavily invested in our platform and minimizing the integration work done by our developers," he says. "We want to make sure we do everything we can to support our ecosystem."[16] He feels the risk is low of ecosystem partners working against each other. "We don't see it as a competition," he remarks. "Our goals are very well-aligned. If an external developer writes an amazing app that gets a lot of adoption, that's amazing for us. It means our value went up without having to build it ourselves."[17] Slack keeps close relationships with its partners: "We have taken third-party developers to customer pitches."[18] In some cases, they have even acquired partners, such as Missions, which became Slack's Workflow Builders.

One challenge Sahni and his platform colleagues are tackling now is driving more consistency across the portfolio of Slack APIs. When product teams work quickly and independently, it's hard to coordinate standards across the board. Slack has now defined a set of API design guidelines that they share and use to solve this issue. He believes if it had been employed earlier, it would have saved oodles of rework time. "APIs are forever, and changing them is very hard," he explains, in reference to the need for external coordination when significant changes are introduced. "Isn't it worth spending two days now, versus two years fixing things in the future?"[19] The guidelines are now being used effectively and are helping to prevent refactoring of API designs.

Slack's APIs are flourishing, and its platform continues to grow in multiple dimensions: users, apps, features. APIs are at the heart of all of these. Sahni is excited about helping to drive and deal with this growth that first started with the recognition of a happy accident and then flourished through a continual application of the OOOps methods.

OOOps at Slack

- Create **optionality** by allowing third-party developers to directly use unbundled, API-enabled digital services.
- Business development teams identify and exploit **opportunities** by bringing API-enabled partner innovations directly to customer prospects.
- Drive **optimization** by continually examining API consumption and aligning consumption patterns with business opportunities.

With the luxury of hindsight, we can see that the biggest difference between the stories of Flickr and Slack was in the eventual acquisition. Flickr was bought by Yahoo! for $25 million,[20] while Slack went public with a valuation of over $15 billion[21] and was eventually bought by Salesforce for over $27 billion.[22] This order of magnitude difference brings us back to the "10X win" concept at the beginning of this chapter. While it's true to say that Butterfield got lucky in both scenarios, it's also true to say that Butterfield was shrewd enough to see the potential in his happy accidents. Beyond the keen eye of Butterfield, however, there is also his applied learning from the first time around, which not only gave him the confidence to double down and pivot his entire enterprise but also gave him the insight to invest in platform engineering to capitalize on his capabilities and maximize his chances of delivering a 10X game-changing win.

In looking at the examples above, it may seem like this pattern is limited to digital pirates, but like all the other patterns explained in this book, there are multiple examples of storied enterprises boldly making their own luck with this pattern of unbundling and capitalizing. One such organization stands out as a consistent leader with an appetite to rewrite its organizational DNA to embrace the possibility of remaking itself as an enterprise with a suite of SaaS offerings: Capital One.

Capital One: Any Organization Can Capitalize on Capabilities...Even Ones That Did Not Create Them

Founded in 1988, Capital One started as a credit card company. Thanks to a sense of conviction that the company could become much more, Capital One has grown into an international financial services enterprise where digital products and technology are not only a core competency but also a differentiator and business development strategy. In 2016, Capital One released a suite of public APIs in a developer portal dubbed DevExchange. This was more than four years before industry regulations like the EU's Payment Services Directive (PSD2) went into full effect to accelerate the open banking revolution.

During our research, several sources noted the willingness of executive leadership at Capital One to focus on recruiting and developing API-specific skills in both the technology and business disciplines.[23] The sustained investment in recruiting and developing talent has set Capital One apart from many financial services organizations. Even in 2023, many of these organizations are still on the fence about the specific business value to be obtained by developing technology-specific skills and offerings within a business-centric discipline and context. The top levels of leadership at Capital One have a detailed and nuanced understanding of how opportunity costs, operational costs, and customer experience all factor into an enterprise view of return on investment.

Brave leadership is not a new thing for Capital One, as their appetite to be a known leader in the financial services industry made them a fintech company before there was even a term for such a thing. Capital One's strategy in becoming a digital player has yet to fully mature, and like a shrewd player, they have multiple bets on the table and are experimenting with several different ways to develop engagement and new revenue opportunities. The DevExchange continues to be a robust portal of digital widgets to create products and offerings on top of Capital One's platform. Separately, to take one more step into the operating model of a software company, Capital One has leaned into its own strengths of rapidly turning data into insight and partnered with a newer digital pirate, Snowflake, to help other enterprises tackle the problem of solving data management challenges at scale.

The decades of consistent investment in cutting-edge approaches, cloud technologies, APIs, and microservices have delivered near-term operational wins, like being able to compress massive financial portfolio migrations from acquisitions that used to take months down to a couple of days. As Capital One Senior Director David Harmony said, "adding 15 million new customers is now a standard day-to-day operation."[24] It is this operational excellence that has culminated in the transformation of Capital One into a true software and services player as they launched their new B2B SaaS offering, Capital One Software, in June of 2022 to help enterprises scale up their use of data and cloud computing.

While there is not yet sufficient clarity and market adoption of the newly released software offerings to declare this transformation effort a success, there are some early signs that Capital One has the sophistication to make this bet pay off. Given that Capital One has the conviction to use its own offerings at scale (what Steve Yegge referred to as "the Golden Rule of platforms"[25]), they've been able to take that hard-earned confidence to market. ThoughtSpot, one of Capital One's early adopters, has expressed confidence in the offering, stating, "I would be more worried about [using a product from] a Series A startup…than I would using [one from] Capital One."[26]

Even if it takes some time for this option to mature, that is not necessarily a bad sign given that Capital One's CEO, Rich Fairbanks, is lauded for consistently taking Capital One "into businesses that have compressed margins and driven up costs in the short term, only to pay off handsomely over time"[27] and has been cited by JPMorgan analyst Rick Shane for "having the confidence and success to support and invest in his vision [based upon] those prior successes."[28]

It is not just Fairbanks who has the long-term mindset grounded in optionality and transformation. Capital One's CIO, Rob Alexander, has the same level of conviction and steadfastness, stating, "We go into this with… humility about the challenge of building a software company. If you look at the average [enterprise] software business, the time it takes to get to $100 million in revenue is, like, five to seven years for the winners. We recognize that this is something we need to be in for the long term."[29]

While there may be some skeptics out there who look at this attempt to capitalize on their capabilities as losing focus on their core markets and capabilities, this specific criticism doesn't seem to pass a basic pressure test given Capital One's recent acquisition of Discover. This acquisition will again leverage their hard-won expertise at digitally integrating acquisitions to pair Capital One's credit card business with a payment network that is now in-house (allowing Capital One to save a projected $1.5 billion in operating expenses).[30]

OOOps at Capital One

- Create **optionality** and enable technology partners to utilize Capital One's digital capabilities via API-enabled digital services.
- Business and IT jointly identify **opportunities** by building and mining their own digital capabilities and matching them up with acquisition opportunities and cross-industry pain points.
- Drive **optimization** and continuous improvement through a mix of operational excellence and grounding their decisions on an ever-improving data-to-insight infrastructure.

Think Big, Start Small, Learn Fast, Go Far

This strategy of unbundling and capitalizing on once-buried capabilities is not unique to Slack or Capital One. Multiple enterprises, like Amazon, Google, Coca-Cola, and others, have utilized this pattern to create new categories of uncapped value. Before moving on to other patterns, it is worth a second look to compare the cases with enterprises that did not choose to unbundle and capitalize at a time when they might have had the opportunity.

Looking back to Chapter 5, we covered Etsy's OOOps moment while paving their feedback loops (feature flags, ramps, and visualization tools). While we don't necessarily know if or how the decisions to unbundle their feature flag and A/B testing capabilities inside Etsy were made, we have the luxury of hindsight to see the potential value of a targeted offering in this space. In the time since Etsy first started sharing its advanced DevOps capabilities with the world, multiple organizations in the last decade have placed their bets on bringing products to market to help organizations manage the complexities of multivariate testing.

- **Optimizely:** Founded in 2010 by a team that came out of Google, Optimizely was supported by Y Combinator and angel investors. The company became cash flow positive in 2011 and was acquired by Episerver in 2020 for nearly $600 million.[31]
- **LaunchDarkly:** Founded in 2014 by Edith Harbaugh of TripIt and John Kodumal of Atlassian, LaunchDarkly has been through several rounds of fundraising and is estimated to have collected $57 million of revenue in 2022. Per their last round of funding, LaunchDarkly is valued at $3 billion.[32]
- **ExactTarget (now known as Salesforce Marketing Cloud):** ExactTarget was founded in late 2000 by Scott Dorsey, Chris Baggott, and Peter McCormick. The firm achieved profitability with revenues exceeding $41 million in 2006 and went public in 2012. ExactTarget was acquired by Salesforce.com in 2013 for $2.5 billion.[33]

It's important to note here that this specific phenomenon (i.e., choosing to pass on unbundling and capitalizing) is not limited to Etsy. Throughout the last two decades, we've seen companies like Yahoo!, Netflix, and others succeed at generating a community of interest by openly sharing their technology tools (e.g., Yahoo! with Hadoop and YUI, and Netflix with OSS, Chaos Monkey, and others) but fail to turn that community of interest to their external financial advantage (beyond gaining access to a talent pipeline).

Conversely, we've also seen shrewd players like Amazon, Capital One, and Slack take things they've perfected for their own use and turn them into money-making powerhouses that also empower and deliver value to a wide community. As we finish writing this book, we've seen Spotify leverage its own digital expertise and lean in on a new digital offering called Backstage in an as-of-yet uncertain attempt to capture B2B revenue from enterprises looking to optimize developer productivity and software delivery with the use of robust and easy-to-operate developer portals.

10X Wins Don't Require 10X Investment to Get Started

Within this chapter, we've covered what is perhaps the most exciting of the four strategies of success. The 10X wins from Amazon and Slack are truly compelling. It is important to remember two things. First, none of the organizations mentioned in this chapter saw their investments in technology as a passing fancy or another shiny object to chase after. In each story, the executives created a sense of focus and urgency to build the teams, skills, processes, and leadership that allow a company to break lanes and become a force outside of the context where it is comfortable. Second, none of the successful companies looked to bet big out of the gate. They all started small and leveraged what they were good at to manage risk and work through the challenges of learning how to operate in a new market context, where each of the three OOOps methods came together to help them rapidly navigate and thrive where others did not dare to go.

In the next chapter, we'll explore the last of the four success strategies and learn how two enterprises repeatedly found ways to create new tiers of value opportunity by aggregating and connecting data and capabilities from across their enterprises.

9

Strategies of Success #4: Value Aggregation

In this chapter, we will examine the last of our unbundling success strategies: *value aggregation*. In this strategy, organizations use the OOOps methods to connect business models within their ecosystem. They use APIs as connection points between the models, use value dynamics to identify the opportunities for value network aggregation, and then adopt a "whole is greater than the sum of its parts" mentality to further optimize the landscape.

To demonstrate the strategy, we will show how digital pirate Google turned its Maps product into a channel for its other business lines, and we'll also look at how digital settler Best Buy combined retail sales with its Geek Squad repair business. In addition to the OOOps methods, these stories highlight the importance and uniqueness of data as a currency of value exchange. With that in mind, let's briefly dig into the potential of data before studying the examples.

Data Economics

The digital economy is largely a data economy. The digital pirates we cite frequently—Amazon, Google, Meta/Facebook—are often referred to as "Big Tech." However, there is a strong argument to be made that it is data that fuels and differentiates each of their business models. In the early days of

Amazon, when the company was primarily an online book retailer, its staff included full-time book reviewers. This group was let go when the company realized the review data it collected from customers drove more sales. Google correlated web activity with user profiles to build a multibillion-dollar advertising business. We've already discussed how Facebook took this a step further in its overt collection of personal data and how that unleashed its successful business model. It was the same story for next-generation digital pirates like Uber (data-based ride matching with no full-time drivers or cars) and Netflix (hyper-personalized show recommendations). Data is now fueling the AI revolution.

These digital pirates recognize that data is a business asset, not just a technical one. As the cost of storing and processing data has decreased, and its utility has become more apparent, digital settlers are also becoming keenly aware of data's value. Economists have acknowledged that data breaks many standard economic assumptions that were established in the physical goods economic paradigm. In economic terms, data is a *non-rival, non-fungible, experience good*. Let's unpack each of these traits.

Non-Rival Goods

We've already covered the economic idea of rivalrous versus non-rivalrous goods when discussing digital products. A rival good is one that can only be possessed or consumed by a single user, whereas a non-rival good can be consumed or held by users simultaneously. A piece of birthday cake is a rivalrous good. The song "Happy Birthday"—which can be sung (poorly) by many people at once—is non-rival. As pointed out previously, there is no linear relationship between the unit cost and consumption of a non-rival product, meaning the return on investment for a non-rival good can be exponentially large.

Non-Fungible Goods

A good is considered fungible if its units are swappable. Non-fungible goods are those whose units are sufficiently unique so that they cannot be substituted. To an artist like Bob Ross, a paintbrush is fungible, but the artist's paintings are not. Due to their irreplaceability, non-fungible goods can carry very large valuations and give tremendous leverage to their holders.

Experience Goods

When the value of a product or service is not known until it has been consumed, it is an experience good. The opposite of an experience good is a search good, one whose value can be determined prior to consumption. A haircut is an experience good. The hat you buy to cover up a bad haircut would be a search good.

Interestingly, the availability of data on what would previously be considered experience goods—restaurants, hotels, used items—is pushing many of them closer to becoming search goods.

More notably for the economic discussion, there can be a wide variance in the perceived value of experience goods depending on the consumer's context. This means that a value exchange involving experience goods can look like a rip-off in hindsight, even though both parties were happy in the first place.

Positive Externalities

There is another economic phenomenon when it comes to data. Accumulating more data makes the data you already have even more valuable. And the more you collect, the more you understand the data you have, which increases its value even more. These effects are called *positive externalities* in economic terms. By gaining more correlation between the data you have and being able to put it in context, these abilities drive an exponential increase in the data's value.

To sum up, as an economic asset, data is a non-rival, non-fungible, experience good whose accumulation leads to positive externalities. The next time someone claims that "data is the new oil," you can tell them they couldn't be more wrong. Oil is the exact opposite of data: a rival, fungible, search good. This summary is depicted in Figure 9.1.

The point of all this is to illustrate the significance of data to the success of organizations in the digital economy. More specifically for the unbundling approach we describe, data is how disparate value networks can be connected. Sharing data across different lines of business is what enables the value aggregation strategy we discuss in this chapter.

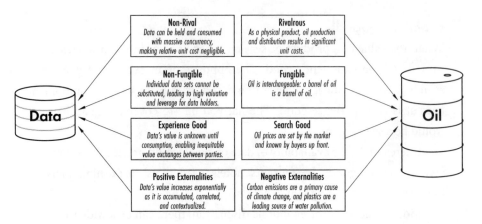

FIGURE 9.1: The Economic Properties of Data vs. Oil

Data Can Connect Value Networks

In Chapter 4, we learned about value networks, value dynamics, and how to create maps that represent value exchanges within a value network. The truth is that most enterprises operate within many value networks. Within the constraints of pre-digital business, operations for each value network might be organizationally separate and operationally isolated. An automotive company's manufacturing arm operated at a distance from its dealer network. A bank's retail and commercial banking divisions each operated independently. In the digital age, data has the potential to remove many of the barriers that led to this isolation.

The savviest digital pirates have already figured this out. Amazon started with a grand retail vision but began operations with a focus on selling books. Through the purchases of readers in their book-centered value network, they were able to collect data on the interests of their customers that could be leveraged as they expanded into the sales of new product categories. Later, they were able to use similar individualized data to build an audience of media streamers through their Prime Video service. Facebook convinced more than a billion people to upload their personal data to its data stores so that it could then be shared with close family members and long-lost friends. The data from the value network of social interactions turned to gold when connected to the company's nascent value network of advertising. Connecting the value networks was the key to the long-term success and growth of these digital pirates.

We call this strategy of using data to connect value networks *value aggregation*. When done well, this pattern can have a *1+1=3* effect for the organizations using it. That effect can be explained by each of data's economic properties we articulated above:

- **Non-rivalry:** Connecting value networks through data leads to more opportunity for consumption of that data with no incremental production costs.
- **Non-fungibility:** Broader access to unique data inside an organization leads to more economic leverage for the organization.
- **Experience good:** More opportunity to utilize the data within the organization raises the relative value of the data.
- **Positive externalities:** Connected value networks create more opportunity to correlate the connected data and use the data in new contexts, thereby exponentially increasing its value.

Let's now look at two examples where enterprises—one a digital pirate and one a digital settler—utilized value aggregation to great effect.

From Mapping to Marketing at Google

We've looked at Google Maps from a few perspectives thus far, but let's now consider it in the context of value aggregation. Google Maps started out as a web application aimed at people browsing the internet. The announcement blog post touted services like directions and "nearby search." Users did not need to pay to use Google Maps, but usage of the service allowed Google to collect information on location-based interests and activities. This original value exchange map for Google Maps is depicted in Figure 9.2.

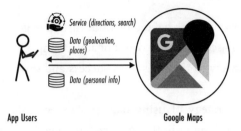

FIGURE 9.2: Google Maps Business Model in 2005

Within months of Maps launching, industrious users had reverse engineered its underlying API to build map-based apps of their own. As discussed previously, Google embraced this move and launched the Maps API in June of 2005. This new channel created a medium for value exchange with third-party developers who could provide their own data to Google in return for geolocation data, place information, and directions and search services. Those app developers could then use the services and data provided by the Google Maps API to augment their apps with geolocation capabilities to help drive their own value exchanges with their users. Over time, Google imposed tier-based pricing on the API to recover costs that were driven by a small percentage of users. Figure 9.3 illustrates what the Google Maps business model looked like around 2006.

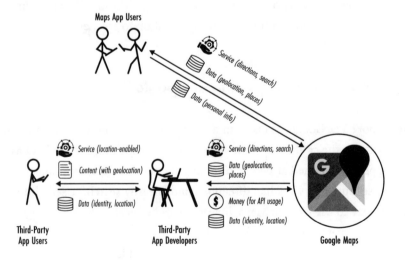

FIGURE 9.3: Google Maps Business Model in 2006

As the Maps service—both app and API—matured, Google was able to connect it with its core search service as well as its Ads cash cow to really drive the business model. Third-party businesses could list themselves on Maps, allowing them to reach the Maps app users as well as users of apps that were enhanced through the Google Maps API. Furthermore, these businesses could buy ads to have their businesses show up higher in search results lists. Figure 9.4 shows how Google was able to leverage these core capabilities from multiple product areas to drive a comprehensive business model in terms of value exchange.

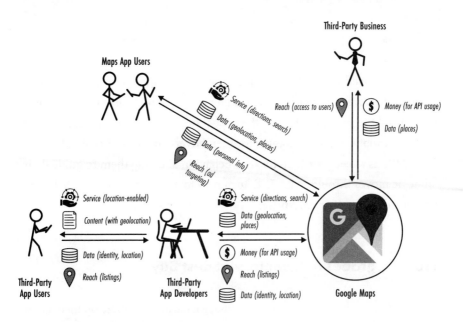

FIGURE 9.4: Google Maps Business Model in 2011

From this illustration, you can see how Google could and did make subsequent moves to connect YouTube, Android, and other platforms in their ecosystem to create even more powerful value exchanges. It is clear from this illustration how Google has effectively employed value aggregation to devastating effect in their growth and web dominance.

OOOps at Google

- Create **optionality** by unbundling geolocation data services from web app UI.
- Discover new **opportunities** for value exchange between mobile channel, location data, and ad network.
- Optimize service delivery and revenue **opportunities** by using APIs as a method of instrumentation.

Google used unbundling to open their geolocation services via API in response to developer demand. Through value dynamics–like thinking, they recognized the power of APIs in the post-iPhone mobile explosion and used Maps on mobile as a new channel for their advertising business. Finally, they used APIs as a feedback loop for user behavior, allowing them to guide their strategic moves through data. Let's turn now to an example of value aggregation at a digital settler enterprise.

From Upgrades to Inventory at Best Buy

As we related earlier in the book, in 1966, Richard M. Schulze opened a new electronics store in his hometown of St. Paul, Minnesota, named Sound of Music. After he spent fifteen years modestly growing the business, a tornado tore the roof off the biggest Sound of Music location. To try and make up for his losses, Schulze promoted a huge "Tornado Sale" featuring "best buys" on all remaining merchandise. The successful sale set the stage for the company to change its name to Best Buy and to focus on low prices and high volume.

Schulze didn't stop there. In retrospect, the tornado seemingly set Best Buy spinning with a culture of introspection and innovation. While many of its Midwest electronics competitors struggled in the late 1980s and early 1990s, Best Buy expanded its product lines and regional coverage, powered by new store concepts and supply chain optimization. Given this appetite for experimentation, it is no surprise that Best Buy welcomed rather than feared the rise of the World Wide Web and e-commerce in the late 1990s.

BestBuy.com launched in 2000, and its annual report from that year speaks of its confidence to "meet our customers at the intersection of technology and life" and its identity as a "consumer-centric company."[1] In the early 2000s, Best Buy went all in on this "consumer-centric" approach under new CEO Brad Anderson, helping the company successfully navigate shifting consumer behaviors while competitors like Circuit City fell to the wayside.

At the dawn of the smartphone boom in 2007/2008, Best Buy once again made a shrewd move to see this not only as a new commercial opportunity to sell products but also as an opportunity to establish more effective channels to connect with customers and suppliers. Personal mobile devices presented the perfect opportunity to realize the company's customer-centric vision. The Apple App Store triggered a digital gold rush as app developers clamored to reach consumers. Best Buy recognized that the picks and shovels required by these app prospectors were web APIs that could be used to provide data and services and embed Best Buy's presence. The company budgeted a bold initiative, "TAG Superhighway," to create a platform for those web APIs.

At that time, BestBuy.com was operating separately from the main company. Although Best Buy had seen huge potential reward in the dot-com boom at the turn of the millennium, they had also seen high risk. To mitigate that, its leaders had created BestBuy.com as a separate company, in a different office, and even in a different city from their corporate headquarters. This covered the risk and allowed BestBuy.com to develop its own culture, featuring close collaboration between marketers and technologists. There was no concept of IT at the dot-com entity, no isolation of technical work from business activities. "That kind of DNA allowed BestBuy.com to be more experimental," recalls Ian Kelly, who was BestBuy.com's director of engineering at the time.[2]

BestBuy.com's resulting success brought recognition from the parent company in the form of new responsibility. Kelly and his team were tasked with creating an innovation platform for the whole enterprise. This platform was intended to house the core capabilities that would provide a digital foundation for Best Buy. It enabled the company to quickly launch new products and services or to exploit new customer and supplier channels. The new platform reused some ingredients from the work already done at BestBuy.com —a set of APIs known as "Remix" created by the marketing team.

One of the first initiatives that utilized the platform was a buyback program. When customers bought their electronic devices (like laptops and phones), Best Buy would offer to repurchase them at a future date, say two years. Best Buy would also offer an extended warranty for the ownership term. This program was a win for customers, who knew the devices would be out of date by the end of the term, and a win for Best Buy, which had greater certainty of future revenue as well as recurring revenue through the warranties sold. However, the biggest beneficiary of the new service was the team that had come up with the idea in the first place: Geek Squad.

At that time, Geek Squad—Best Buy's electronics repair service—had one of the biggest inventories of consumer electronics in the world but was always in need of parts to replenish their supply. Using the API-enabled digital platform, Kelly and a team of six were able to stand up the new service in three weeks. This rapid delivery was made possible by existing APIs on the platform, as well as by accessing external APIs to outsource the warranty and logistics services.

Let's examine this buyback program through the lens of value dynamics. In the early 2000s, Best Buy was already undergoing digital transformation in several directions. Its operations were being digitized, it was exploring e-commerce through BestBuy.com, and it was also servicing a huge demand for web-capable consumer electronics. Best Buy's Geek Squad service became a leader in PC and electronics repair and required a massive inventory of parts to keep up with demand.

At the dawn of the mobile boom triggered by the launch of the iPhone in 2007, Best Buy's brick-and-mortar store locations were running on all cylinders in the sales and servicing of consumer electronics. Best Buy's business model was straightforward, collecting money for product sales and for servicing electronics through Geek Squad. This business model is depicted in Figure 9.5.

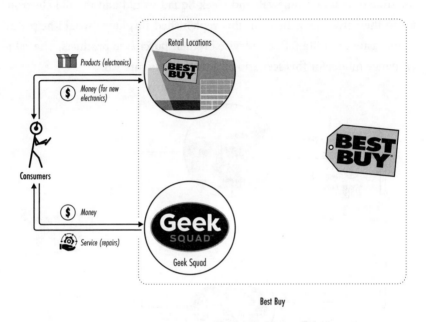

Best Buy

FIGURE 9.5: Best Buy Store Business Model in 2007

As the first decade of the 2000s came to a close, Best Buy had concurrent issues in each of these two revenue streams. In sales, retaining customers had become challenging in the highly competitive smartphone business. Based on network subscriptions, customers needing to replace their phones after two years were likely to go elsewhere to look for the best deal. Best Buy wanted to find a way to improve the retention of these customers. In terms of services, Geek Squad had a more straightforward problem: inventory. They were in constant need of products and parts to deal with overwhelming demand. By creating APIs on its digital platform, Best Buy was able to launch their buy-back program, which created a "win-win-win" situation for Geek Squad, Best Buy stores, and Best Buy's customers.

As we related earlier, at the time of purchasing a new phone (or other electronics), a customer could sign up to have Best Buy repurchase their phone at the end of their contract term, thus guaranteeing they would recoup some of their money. Best Buy would guarantee an in-store customer visit at the time of contract renewal, and Geek Squad would add the old electronics to their inventory. In turn, this replenished inventory would help Best Buy's customers obtain faster service on their purchased products. The value exchange model for this scenario is depicted in Figure 9.6.

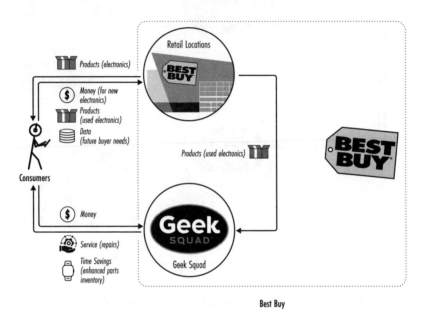

FIGURE 9.6: Best Buy Store Business Model in 2012

This value aggregation example is just one of the successes Best Buy experienced through their unbundling approach. Using their Remix API platform, the company overhauled its recommendations engine and realized a $10 million return on investment in year one.[3]

Another successful initiative was the development of a digital analog to Best Buy's newspaper flyers. For years, Best Buy's largest electronics providers had paid for promotional space in flyers handed out in Sunday newspapers, effectively subsidizing the high print and distribution costs. With the decline of print media and the rise of digital, Best Buy created a Deals web service that cost its partners one-tenth the price of print and allowed for targeting and real-time measurement of impact. The service itself was built by using APIs that were already on their platform, such as product and pricing services. "It paid for itself in a month," says Kelly.[4] These digitally enabled business innovations helped Best Buy not just survive, but thrive in a volatile industry during a period of heavy disruption.

OOOps at Best Buy

- Create **optionality** through a platform of building block APIs for external and internal consumption.
- Business and IT teams identify **opportunities** and run centrally funded experiments.
- Relentless **optimization** by focusing on short-term ROI rather than net costs.

Make Your Own Treasure Maps

Value aggregation may be the most powerful of the success strategies we have discussed so far. Its adoption is certainly one of the practices that differentiates the most successful digital pirates from other enterprises. However, each of the other patterns we discussed—exchange optimization, distributed innovation, and capability capitalization—should all be considered as you look to benefit from the implementation of the OOOps methods at your organization. And these are by no means the only success patterns available. Many more will follow.

At this point, you have learned the methods of the unbundling approach, as well as several success patterns. Let's turn now to some practical considerations that are essential to find your digital treasure.

PRACTICAL
CONSIDERATIONS
TO FINDING
DIGITAL
TREASURE

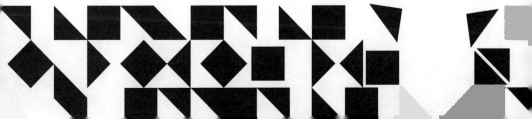

Within Parts I and II, we unpacked each of the three OOOps methods and then, with real-world use cases, showed how these methods can be used in concert to execute each of the four treasure-hunting strategies. In Part III, we will shift our focus toward a set of practical concerns including:

- **Getting started:** We'll cover the basics for how to get started with an unbundling initiative and ensure that you are prepared to handle objections from across your enterprise. Beyond helping you overcome initial objections, we'll also ensure that you are fluent and familiar with all the tips and tricks necessary to achieve scaled results quickly without sacrificing enterprise compliance requirements.
- **Risk identification and mitigation:** We'll provide you with a robust unbundling risk management reference sheet that includes strategies for detection and mitigation.
- **Planning with uncertainty in mind:** We'll take a closer look at how the future is unfolding itself in front of us all right now. We will give you the context to understand how APIs and unbundling are the main forces driving these current events and help you connect these events to your plans for creating and conserving options of your own.

Finally, we'll wrap up the book with our conclusion and give you a telescope to see what's on the horizon as the current of the digital seas pushes us all to an inescapable path of least resistance.

10

Getting Started on the Path
to Scaled Results

I n this chapter, we will examine the areas that are essential for organizations that want to get started with an unbundling initiative along with an elaboration of the grounding concepts that will ultimately keep your program on the path to scaled results. While we know you're eager to get started on your adventure to the land of a thousand shovels, if it's scaled financial impact you're after, there are a few more tools we'll have to put in your digital pirate kit. Most importantly, you'll need to know the ins and outs of a default-to-open approach.

Moving from Organization to Ecosystem

Throughout this book, we have presented examples of organizations that have used APIs to achieve success in the digital economy. In some of these examples, such as Lowe's and Coca-Cola, the APIs are only consumed internally. In other examples, such as Cox and Google Maps, APIs are directly web-facing and are often consumed by third-party organizations. To play the digital long game and capture scaled financial impact, there is growing evidence that the future will require external APIs to plug into the web-based ecosystems of digital business.

One of the tenets of Jeff Bezos's API mandate was that all of Amazon's services needed to be "designed from the ground up to be externalizable."[1] Given the arguments that Tim O'Reilly presented to Bezos in 2002 served, at least in part, to convince him to adopt APIs—the power of a platform strategy, crowdsourced innovation, new revenue opportunities—it seems likely that Bezos's focus was always on the opportunities presented by external APIs. The productivity and scaling benefits Amazon gained from their unbundling approach were significant, but the complementary benefit of positioning the company as a vital platform in the burgeoning web economy was also essential.

Bezos was not the only one to see this future. Between 1999 and 2004, John Hagel III, veteran of both McKinsey and Deloitte, produced several prophetic works, including the *Harvard Business Review* article "Unbundling the Corporation" (with coauthor Marc Singer) and the 2004 book *Out of the Box*. Hagel's work foretold the rise of industry-aligned "infomediaries," companies that serve as information brokers and service providers directly to customers (e.g., AutoTrader.com, Yelp, TripAdvisor, etc.) and pointed to the likelihood of Amazon pioneering the IaaS category.[2]

The mobile, social, and cloud booms between 2007 and 2010 were significantly enabled by web APIs. During this time, API-driven growth was well understood for Facebook, Amazon, Apple, Netflix, Google (often referred to as "the FAANGs"), and many others. Beyond the examples of the FAANGs, two API product companies that emerged in 2008 are worth examining more closely: Twilio and Stripe.

Telecommunications companies had been early providers of web APIs, providing carrier services like telephony, messaging, and billing to drive interoperability in the industry. The iPhone launch in 2007 created a gold rush for app developers, and these telco functions would be ideal services to build into their apps. Still, a developer building global apps might need to connect with dozens of carriers. On top of that, API formats and protocols were inconsistent across the carriers, and ease of use was lacking.

Twilio saw this market opportunity and created their own API-based product. In one sense, they did this by unbundling, since the product consisted of discrete, digitally accessible telco capabilities. In another sense, they were bundling since they were able to aggregate the regional providers into a global offering. Twilio took the offering a step further by focusing on developer experience, based on their recognition that in the market dynamics of the mobile boom, time to market and lower complexity were valuable enough to justify increased usage costs.

Stripe followed a similar path to Twilio in a different industry, unbundling the payment functions required by app developers and bundling their disparate providers. This collective approach was an API analog to the retail-wholesale model for physical goods. Both companies provided a targeted marketplace for service providers. Both companies were also wildly successful, growing to multibillion-dollar valuations rapidly with very little infrastructure investment required. These API-specific examples were part of a larger trend in platform businesses overall.

After a decade of progress in the API economy, the 2016 book *Platform Revolution*, by Sangeet Paul Choudary, Marshall Van Alstyne, and Geoffrey G. Parker, included a close-up study of companies like Uber, Airbnb, and PayPal that had established a digital business model around two-sided marketplaces and network effects. (A two-sided, or N-sided, marketplace is an intermediary economic platform with multiple distinct user groups. The operators of these multi-sided marketplaces provide "matchmaking" services to market participants by connecting suppliers with consumers.)

The book introduces the concept of an "inverted firm,"[3] synonymous with Hagel and Singer's "infomediaries." Inverted firms create platforms that capture value by intermediating value exchanges between third parties. The book contrasts this platform approach with the traditional "pipeline" approach of old-school manufacturing organizations that create value in steps along a controlled production process. The book also shows how APIs play a central role in digital intermediation for platform companies.

Van Alstyne, along with Seth Benzell and Jonathan Hersh, followed up the work on platform economics with a study published in 2023 showing the economic impact of API adoption for organizations. Titled "How APIs Create Growth by Inverting the Firm," the paper includes significant findings with respect to the impact of public—that is external—APIs. According to their research, "firms adopting public APIs grew an additional 38.7% over sixteen years relative to similar non-adopters."[4] The study shows that growth is not limited to a longer time scale, as market value of public firms grew "an additional 12.9% versus similar firms two years after [public API] adoption."[5] The authors use specific analysis to conclude that the relationship between APIs and firm growth is causal, not just correlated. Despite performing similar analysis on organizations using APIs internally, the study finds no statistically significant relationship between internal API adoption and firm performance. The paper is clear in its conclusion: organizations that want to benefit the most from APIs should be focusing on externalizing APIs.

The real-world evidence of Van Alstyne's claim is on display across multiple industries and geographic boundaries. This is not to say that the concept of disruptive unbundling is only restricted to APIs. This tactic has been around for decades. At the turn of the millennium, Oracle is said to have unbundled IBM.[6] Soon thereafter, Yahoo! unbundled AOL, Google unbundled Yahoo!, and Facebook unbundled Google.[7] This story has repeated itself over and over with examples ranging from music (via Napster, Apple, and streaming services like Spotify), transportation (via Tesla, ride-sharing, scooters, etc.), money (via blockchain-enabled digital currencies), and space (via SpaceX, Blue Origin, etc.).

A key distinction in the realm of APIs is that the use of externalized APIs dramatically reduces the effort needed in any future efforts to unbundle or bundle existing offerings. This inverse relationship between the presence of externally available, decomposed capabilities and the cost of introducing new bundled/unbundled offerings is the specific reason that APIs have perhaps the most powerful leverage available in an organization's attempts to create and conserve optionality.

Several of the examples given in this book—AWS, Google Maps, Slack, Cox—bear this out. Since Twilio and Stripe set the pattern, the number of successful API product companies continues to grow: Nylas in communications, Plaid in banking, Symbl.ai in natural language processing, Agora in voice processing. There are even ecosystem opportunities for regional businesses to operate. Okra is a Nigerian startup that is taking advantage of an entire continent that is routinely underbanked.[8] As a result, Okra is focused on providing unbundled banking services via APIs to app developers across the African continent to help pave the financial infrastructure needed for regional economic growth. According to Okra's cofounder, Fara Ashiru Jituboh, "Our goal is to ensure the continent of Africa can compete in the fourth Industrial Revolution, and the impact of data cannot be overstated."[9] Every business needs to consider where the opportunities for ecosystem advantage exist in their industries and regions.

A deep dive into a comprehensive view on the best practices for externalizing APIs would warrant a book of its own. There are many considerations for launching and managing external APIs, and we have captured many of them throughout the book, from strategy to design to implementation. As your organization begins to define its approach to API product management, you will want to review the set of considerations we have captured in Table 10.1 There are many more considerations than these, and many online resources and tools to help you on your journey as an external API provider, as well as a consumer. Nonetheless, this list should help you start thinking through the journey as you transform the perspective of your organization from a bounded entity to a constituent in a broad digital ecosystem.

TABLE 10.1: Considerations for API Providers

Public API Product Strategy	• What consumers are you targeting with your API and why do they want/need it? • What is the vision for the capabilities offered by the API? • What value are you planning to deliver/capture? • Do you have internal alignment between your stakeholders and delivery teams? • What KPIs will you measure and track to optimize your products?
Public API Launch Strategy	• Do you have partners you want to launch with? • How and where will you market the API? • What functionality and features will be in the MVP?

Pricing/ Finance Strategy	• What is the business model for your API? • What type of pricing approach will you take? Tiered? Usage-based? Segmented? Free/freemium? • How does your ROI model account for the non-rival nature of your product? • Do you have internal alignment on investing to lower the cost of experiments?
Developer Experience (DX)	• How will developers discover the API? • How will your internal developers and business units make their APIs available? • How will you make the developer experience sticky yet seamless? • How will developers test your product and give you feedback? • What KPIs will you measure and track to optimize DX? • How will you communicate the need for future changes to the consumers of your APIs?
Persona Development & Use	• Is there a difference between the users of your products and the buyers of your products? • What customer roles are influencers in the process of deciding to use and pay for your API products? • How do buyers see and quantify the value of your product when comparing your service to alternatives and substitutes?
Governance Model	• How will you secure the API and protect your data? • What metrics are required? • How will changes be managed at the infrastructure level? At the product level? • How will your product and technology teams collaborate to align on and enforce a set of standards for your API products?

One cautionary finding (discussed in more depth in the following section) was unearthed in the API study from Van Alstyne, Benzell, and Hersh. According to the paper, "firms with public APIs see significantly increased risk of hack events in the years after opening an API."[10] While this does not negate the fact that APIs are an engine for economic growth, this finding does raise an important point that is worth examining more deeply: What are the areas that organizations need to address in order to ensure safe, scalable, and resilient API adoption?

To Win the Game, You Have to Know the Rules

So far, we've covered the incredible power that comes with committing to initiatives on APIs, composability, and optionality. While we have also covered cultural and technical requirements necessary to make these types of initiatives work, what we have not covered are the constraints that these types of initiatives must work within. Regulatory and risk management issues are real things in the enterprise context and ignoring them with a flippant perspective on the potential consequences is not an enterprise-ready strategy.

To get a better handle on how to think about compliance in the context of API-driven optionality, let's look at the firsthand experiences of a digital leader who's had to manage these concerns in a high-profile context.

Of all the leaders we interviewed for this book, Sanjna Verma, currently a user protection product leader at Google, has had the most exposure to the widest variety of risk and legal concerns that come from enabling API access across a wide ecosystem. Prior to managing user privacy concerns within Google, Verma spent several years helping to build multiple parts of the MuleSoft iPaaS (integration platform-as-a-service) product offering that aids enterprises in building and managing an API ecosystem and became a key player in the evolution of Plaid, arguably the most impactful API player in the fintech world.

Some people play checkers and take the next advantageous move that's right in front of them. Some people play chess and orient themselves on a longer-term strategy that has multiple moving parts. Others, like Sanjna

Verma, see the global tapestry of opportunities and challenges and yearn to own the whole board, i.e., Verma plays Risk. Verma immerses herself in regionalized legal contexts and market conditions with an eye to strategically use her resources in ways that account for the regionalized constraints.

Verma led the API-centric offering for COVID-19 tracing in Salesforce's efforts to help the world return to normal during the pandemic. In that time, Verma wrestled with the nuanced details of balancing between US regulatory concerns of healthcare data sharing for individuals and the large-scale concerns of making a pandemic-racked world safe for anyone and everyone to return to. If helping to define and launch the COVID-19 data platform for use by schools and universities, federal and state government institutions, and public and private companies wasn't enough, the impact of Verma's offering spread beyond Earth as she helped bring the offering to NASA as well. The world of public health is one of the most complex games any technology professional can engage with. On the scientific side, precision is everything, while on the public communications side, being precise is often at odds with the charters of institutions, given that complex answers can often lead to disengagement from initiatives designed to reduce mortality rates.

The risk factors Verma had to balance were dizzying:

- Being a profit-driven enterprise while crafting a product with a significant component of altruism, including free and open access to any consumers who wanted to leverage the data.
- Working with institutions that were entrusted with protecting the lives of customers and staff, teachers and students, parents and children, viscerally essential workers, and the all-too-invisible workers inside supply chains.
- Working with organizations around the globe, each with different regulatory and governance frameworks that they were accountable to comply with.

Navigating the international waters of health data sharing taught Verma quite a bit about risk. She took all the lessons and now applies them in the financial sector, which carries similar concerns. In our interview, Verma shared a story where the tightness of US-based regulations on healthcare data are much looser in many parts of the world, while financial data regulations are the mirror image, with extremely tight regulations in the EU and much looser constraints in the US.

After playing in so many different contexts with so many different frameworks and consequences, Verma's approach to managing legal compliance within a high-demand offering is one of careful but determined risk management. Given the global nature of Plaid's offering, it might be tempting to approach product development and go-to-market planning with a "least common denominator" approach that could be universally applicable across markets. However, in our interview, Verma responded to our questions about regulatory concerns by elevating the conversation to a global context. Verma articulated a path where she's both fluent in the regionalized regulatory contexts of different areas of the world and looks to practically apply these different filters both in the ideation process and in the last mile of go-to-market planning.[11]

In the product ideation space, one player might look at a regulatory risk and think it can make certain activities and offerings prohibited, but another player can see the same context and explore that environment for pain points and opportunities to be of value while navigating the tightrope of legal concerns. In the go-to-market space, Verma is quick to jump to the right side of the line and engage legal teams to ensure every boundary is fortified with just the right controls to ensure that no attack surface is left unmanned.

Just-in-Time Compliance

While gig economy companies like Uber and Airbnb aren't what anyone would call paragons of virtue, they have carved a specific path that business and technology leaders shouldn't be quick to dismiss—viewing legal as a tool to be managed rather than as a constraint of business possibilities. Uber's former general counsel, Salle Yoo, took this point of view and was unapologetic about it. "I tell my team, 'We're not here to solve legal problems. We're here to solve business problems. Legal is our tool...I am going to be supportive of innovation,'" Yoo said on a podcast in 2017.[12] Uber's perspective has been seen to be extreme on legal matters, but in our research we found a common point of view that legal compliance was best managed as an advisory function in the go-to-market phase of digital product development rather than a gating function in the ideation and prototyping phases.

The core idea when considering how to enable a balanced mindset on compliance is to remember that legal concerns can be structured along the lines of risk management. Like many engineers, legal professionals can often see their concerns in black and white. What isn't always considered within the conversations with legal stakeholders is how to frame, quantify, and manage compliance risks.

The point of this perspective isn't to say that the legal teams are right or wrong. Rather, the point here is that asking lawyers to make business decisions isn't a good way to frame a request. Rather than asking the legal and compliance teams if you can do something, a more productive question would be along the lines of, "What are the risks involved if we were to engage in X?" or "How might we avoid legal risk if we wanted to engage in X?"

Once business and technology teams are fully versed in the potential risks of a decision, the next step is to make a business decision based upon the likelihood, exposure, and associated trade-offs involved with the options being considered.

When considering this point of view, the classic proverb popularized by pioneering computer scientist Grace Hopper comes to mind: "It is easier to ask for forgiveness than to get permission."[13] A more recent perspective in the same vein was articulated in the earlier referenced Steve Yegge post, where he talks about the balance to be had between accessibility and security. Yegge writes, "I'll argue that Accessibility is actually more important than Security because dialing Accessibility to zero means you have no product at all, whereas dialing Security to zero can still get you a reasonably successful product such as the PlayStation Network."[14]

Taking all these ideas into context, our point here is not to blatantly show a fundamental disrespect for the law and compliance. The tactic to follow is one of balance and not to let legal analysts unilaterally drive business or product strategy. (Unless, by chance, you're building a product for legal audiences, then, by all means, go ahead and do this.)

Given that "achieving balance" can be easier said than done, a north star to follow here is to look to legal to shape your offering rather than approve/deny it. A framework for achieving just-in-time compliance has a handful of basic steps:

- Start by gathering input for where the roadblocks might emerge with a focus on broad legislation/regulation that governs your industry/market (e.g., HIPAA, PCI, GDPR, etc.).
- Once your fusion teams have rough product concepts documented, involve your legal/governance teams to communicate the planned scope of your offerings clearly.
- Shift the frame of conversations from "pass/fail" to either "Please help me shape my offering," or "What would be required to make this offering low risk?"
- Refine your rough offerings to align with compliance concerns.
- Return to legal for complete review prior to full launch.

Before closing the discussion on the need for legal compliance, it is important not to gloss over the need to instill operational guardrails on monitoring/observability (e.g., Who is using my systems? How are my systems behaving? Are they within SLA? Are they spewing errors?) and governability (e.g., applying rate limits to requests, assuring PII is encrypted, assuring that all data accessed is appropriately authorized, etc.) throughout your value streams. These sorts of capabilities are often compared to automotive insurance policies (i.e., The value in the policy is not known until you need it. And when you need it, you'll be glad you have it!). But a more appropriate metaphor would be the safety equipment inside your car (e.g., the brakes, the seat belts, the backup cameras, the rear and side mirrors, the proximity sensors, etc.). The value of safety equipment is in allowing you to travel at high speeds, avoiding incidents altogether, and in the worst-case scenario, protecting you from the most harmful impacts of an unavoidable incident.

In short, launching external API-based offerings without some form of centralized monitoring and governance capabilities is akin to running with scissors. Don't do it.

The Do's and Don'ts of Serial Optionality

Over the course of this book, we've laid out how serial optionality can be achieved via a commitment to modularity and standardized interfaces via APIs and a consistent effort to continually lower the variable cost to execute market-facing experiments. As you embark into this new chapter of transformation, we want to give you a summarized guide with specific guideposts and guardrails for making the most of your efforts to capture the often-stunning effects that can be achieved via APIs and optionality (that is, retaining the right to engage in many different options with no obligation to pursue any of them).

TABLE 10.2: The Do's and Don'ts of Serial Optionality

Do's	*DO commit to unbundling by default:* Always remember that maintaining a disciplined commitment to loosely coupled, decontextualized capabilities is a fundamental prerequisite to maintaining modularity, optionality, and the resulting speed that is necessary to adapt to changes in a volatile marketplace. Tightly coupled capabilities and monolithic applications will always result in calcification of your approach to a market and render you ripe for disruption by a nimble player.
Don'ts	*DON'T engage in framing unbundled capabilities as exclusively internal or external:* Don't forget that framing capabilities as exclusively and forever for internal use cases will not only lock your enterprise out of potential asymmetric benefit from options that could be exploited in unforeseen market opportunities but also raise the probability that they won't be sufficiently secured to prevent an illicit breach by malicious insiders.
Associated Unbundling Methods	*Optionality through APIs:* leverage new financial math and the high-margin power of non-rival products.

Do's	DO commit to being intentional when choosing which interfaces to control and expose: Creating a discipline of mapping your value exchanges is a critical task for business and technology leaders to do together. Not only will this task help align the organization on the dynamics of the business model, but it will also force the organization to be thoughtful on which capabilities and interfaces to invest in and which to spin out or outsource.
Don'ts	DON'T allow business package design to be an afterthought: Packaging and product design are best done in a single step. When digital products are designed and built from a perspective that is divorced from a go-to-market strategy, you're setting yourself up to have to choose between significant rework and leaving money on the table.
Associated Unbundling Methods	Opportunism through value dynamics: approach APIs with a product mindset and leverage value dynamics.

Do's	DO commit to lowering the cost of experiments: Maintaining a "way-of-life" commitment to keeping the end-to-end cost of experimentation low is the key capability that allows for an approach to spread your bets across a wide range of options. When trials have low costs and cycle times, your organization will naturally align to data-driven approaches to develop market fit for its offerings. Conversely, when your cost and time to execute experiments are high, your enterprise will gravitate to experimenting only with a small number of options that are sponsored by those with status and power in the hierarchy.
Don'ts	DON'T be afraid to shut experiments down: In many enterprises, there is a culture where failure is not accepted. Organizations moving to an experimental, learning culture need to break that mental model. If an experiment proves its hypothesis wrong, it is still a successful experiment, not a failure. Make sure you don't spend too much time and money up front building scalability into the experiment assuming the hypothesis will be proven right. Instead, invest in making the experiment as accurately measurable as possible so you draw the right conclusion.
Associated Unbundling Methods	Optimization through feedback loops: create fast feedback loops by cheapening the bets; catalog negative results of experiments to support new financial math.

A Model for Causing and Monetizing Happy Accidents

There are "only two ways to make money in business: One is to bundle; the other is to unbundle."[15] This extremely simple principle was said by Jim Barksdale as a throwaway line in the early nineties as he and Marc Andreessen were finishing up an investor meeting just prior to Netscape's public offering. Since that time, the principle of bundling and unbundling has defined and driven the evolution of digital businesses to much acclaim.

What this quote doesn't reveal are the mechanisms that make bundling and unbundling effective or efficient. Strangely enough, the secret to efficacy in the efforts to rapidly bundle and unbundle at scale isn't so much in the technology that powers digital business models. Rather, when you unpack the Barksdale quip, the fluid definition and structure of an enterprise's product offerings is the foundation that powers both modern and traditional businesses to drive return on investment.

Once you acknowledge that a specific future can't be predicted, the basic premise of being flexible (i.e., having low-cost options) in the face of generic future changes is the commonsense choice to at least hedge your uncertainty. With that foundational concept in place, it's not a great leap to see that systematically (a) placing a large number of low-cost bets and (b) lowering the cost of creating and exploring both current and future options is also the commonsense posture to gain a competitive edge in a turbulent market space.

To see this idea in action, let's look at the automotive industry and the current volatility of the competitive space. Much has changed since Henry Ford first released the Model T. As much as cars have evolved, the industry itself has changed even more. Beyond the successful introduction of new players and sales channels, the industry has transformed from providing automobiles to providing packaged mobility services, meaning that the legacy concepts that make up personal car ownership are looking more and more vulnerable to market erosion and redefinition.

On one hand, Uber and other mobility services enterprises from Lyft to Lime are reframing automotive needs and offerings much in the same way streaming services like Spotify and Pandora reframed what music ownership means to music consumers. While on the other, Tesla is disrupting the industry by extending car ownership with premium bundled features that range from full self-driving as a subscription to enabling "Dog Mode" for the chauffeurs of man's best friend.

As of 2020, in less than the span of twenty years, Uber and Tesla (founded in 2009 and 2003 respectively) jumped from non-existent to being two of the top four most valuable companies in the automotive sector.[16] In 2024, Tesla has the largest market capitalization of any automotive company in the world, and Uber comes in at #3, with a capitalization of close to $146 billion.[17]

Tesla and Uber are building off digital platforms much in the same way that traditional automotive companies built different cars off shared physical platforms. While physical platform sharing has been used in automotive since the 1940s, digital platform sharing is a more recent phenomenon. The successes of Tesla and Uber, along with the successes of the other Big Tech companies, have inspired the automotive incumbents, with Toyota being one of the most notable with multiple bets being placed:

- The highly visible Toyota Connected offering (an example of the distributed innovation strategy) targets both B2C opportunities with individual car owners and B2B opportunities focused on fleet owners.
- The more behind-the-scenes success of opening its finance platform to Mazda and again with Bass Pro Shops (an example of the capability capitalization strategy).

The lesson inside this transformation is that, regardless of industry, both disruptors and incumbents alike need the capability to manage bundled capabilities in a product-centered lens to maintain the agility needed to compete in a rapidly shifting marketplace. Surprisingly, this challenge is most striking and difficult for established enterprises rather than disruptors because established enterprises typically have:

- Existing revenue streams that are at risk of cannibalization.
- Existing staff with vested interest in maintaining the status quo.

- A cornucopia of systems and processes built around a static definition of products, marketing concepts, and bundled offerings.
- A scaled finance team that needs multiple forms of ROI proof before committing to incremental investments.

Despite the larger challenge for existing enterprises, choosing not to embrace a future with capabilities that can be rapidly bundled and unbundled is not an advisable option either, as the barriers to entry in existing markets erode at an ever-increasing pace.

To meet the challenge of digitally enabling newly unbundled capabilities, enterprises must choose their path wisely, not only in product development but also in the wider lens of platform development and product evolution. To help enterprises manage their transition to this new business context, it is important to simplify the concerns to a point that a business or product team can effectively manage them without having to engage in extended efforts in market research and planning (which is often obsolete by the time it is completed).

This puzzle might seem unsolvable until we lower the cost of testing many unbundled/bundled capabilities with real-time market experimentation (i.e., creating and preserving serial optionality with ever-increasing levels of convexity across the full chain of activities inside of a value stream).

Transforming Speed into Cash

Benjamin Franklin was one of the first to articulate the now trite axiom of "time is money."

Remember that time is money. He that can earn ten shillings a day by his labour, and goes abroad, or sits idle one half of that day, though he spends but sixpence during his diversion or idleness, it ought not to be reckoned the only expence; he hath really spent or thrown away five shillings besides.[18]

While Franklin and others who've spoken similar words might have meant to communicate something in between literal and metaphorical, it underlines the importance of making sure you don't miss any time-related measurements. Here are three of the most critical business metrics for a digital transformation that aims to reset the operating model of delivering business value via software:

1. **Time to experiment:** The amount of time (along with required labor and costs) required to expose an experimental delivery of value to the external market.

2. **Time to impactful insight:** The amount of time (along with required labor and costs) required to evaluate the outcome of the experiment with meaningful business implications.

3. **Time to value:** The amount of time (along with required labor and costs) required to realize revenue (or other unit of agreed-upon value) from an experiment.

In the preceding chapters and referenced case studies, we've shown how the three OOOps methods unlock these metrics and the benefits they drive:

1. Scaling modularity via standardized APIs will accelerate enterprise application development and shrink the time to experiment by enabling composability and optionality.

2. Using value dynamics to refine and target your options will help your organization rapidly identify and exploit the most impactful opportunities through serial optionality.

3. Scaling your ability to create and conserve more options by lowering the variable cost of trials at each phase of an experiment will accelerate the process of identifying winning options that can be brought to market and transformed into business executives' favorite metric—OFCF (Operating Free Cash Flow).

The techniques laid out here—unbundling business capabilities into digital building blocks, composing these decontextualized components into products and experiences, opportunistically leveraging optionality—have been proven by digital pirates and used to disrupt established industries. If software is eating the world, as Marc Andreessen put it, then the digital pirates have dined well. However, turning the tables, the very track record of established enterprises in sustainable market performance is something the digital pirates have not yet emulated. As an example, Uber lost $9 billion in 2022.[19] Established enterprises that combine the unbundling approach with their proven success can have an even stronger market advantage than the disruptors.

11

Ensuring a Durable Transformation by Understanding the Risks

Thus far, we've been heads down on the conceptual models, economics, and financial methodologies behind the asymmetric growth that the digital pirates have exploited. In this chapter, we have one last item to add to your digital pirate supply kit (eye patch not included)—an unbundling risk management reference sheet. To help keep your enterprise within a reasonable set of business, technology, and operational guardrails, we've enumerated a specific set of the riskier areas in an unbundling initiative, along with detection and mitigation strategies, for you to be aware of. The specific risks that are likely to come up over the course of an unbundling initiative include:

- increased security risk
- increased performance risk
- increased risk to quality issues
- increased operational complexity
- misapplying the MVP concept
- cannibalizing existing revenue
- technology-centered transformation
- misaligned talent model and processes
- losing discipline in times of compression
- choosing the wrong interface to control
- pervasive use of performative behaviors (aka optionality theater)

In the following sections, we'll go into each of these risks in more detail, including signs to look out for and mitigation strategies.

Increased Security Risk

Risk: An unavoidable consequence of standardizing your digital interfaces for machine-based consumption (i.e., utilizing APIs) is that you are making things simpler for hackers and bad actors to target and exploit. It's just not possible to make things easier for your authorized partners and consumers to engage with without making things easier for hackers to target. Quantitative research, however, has shown that firms with APIs that are widely used in external contexts have a lower frequency of breaches by malicious insiders than enterprises that use APIs in an exclusively internalized context.[1]

Signs to Look For: You'll know this risk requires preventive attention or has unfortunately materialized when:

- Your teams rely on security via obscurity and state that breaches are not likely to occur because you don't publish the locations and addresses of API endpoints.
- Your teams insist that your firm has no public APIs to be concerned about.
- Your enterprise has a bespoke approach to security where individual teams and value streams are expected to come up with an approach that works for their unique context.

Mitigation Strategy: Ensure teams are supplied with the appropriate tools and support to treat security management as non-deferrable scope, with tactics including:

- Be disciplined in your commitment to require teams that make APIs to assume that the APIs will be consumed by external parties at some point in their life span.

- Institutionalize your enterprise's commitment to establishing a layered defense where controls exist at all points of physical, data, and application infrastructure.
- Commit to investments in centralized API-management tools that are not tightly coupled with specific development technology stacks.
- Commit to investments in platform engineering capabilities that centralize the application of security controls on sensitive or proprietary data and content.
- Invest in "shift left" technologies that scan for and identify security vulnerabilities before code is committed to repositories and deployed to production.
- Commit to an absolutist approach to authentication where your enterprise never allows for scaled anonymous API access.

Increased Performance Risk

Risk: Performance and computing efficiency are both intrinsic trade-offs that come with an approach that builds value over an increased number of decoupled components. As the number of handoff points (often referred to as "hops" by technical teams) between different components increases, the inevitable downside is that each one of those handoffs will take time and computing cycles. For the purposes of this book, it's not fully necessary for you to understand the ins and outs of performance profiling and optimization. It's only necessary for you to understand the risk is there, why this particular risk is a "least bad option," how to spot the risk when it is materializing, and what it takes to mitigate it.

Optimizing technical designs for speed of response and computing efficiency above all else is non-productive performance anxiety and is an over-rotation. A distinction to understand in the performance space is that risk of degraded performance and possible increases to the cost of infrastructure are often the preferred risks to have in a scaled enterprise. The performance risks are the preferred risks specifically because they are more easily mitigated than the alternatives (e.g., the time, effort, and cost to work around monolithic applications that have become too rigid for current market conditions can be astronomical when compared with the more manageable costs of incremental infrastructure).

Signs to Look For: You'll know this risk is about to show up or has fully materialized when:

- Your engineering and product teams oversimplify best practice guidance on performance management. A well-known best practice in this space is to leave performance and optimization concerns to later phases of development work to not waste time optimizing systems that may or may not be adopted by consumers. This idea is sometimes used, by less experienced teams, as a justification not to put any effort into anything that is related with optimizing performance.
- Teams are consistently raising the "too many hops" concern (non-productive performance anxiety as referenced previously).
- Teams don't have a sense of how to predict performance changes in different environmental and usage contexts.

Mitigation Strategy: Ensure teams are supplied with the guideposts and support that will help them prepare early and optimize late:

- While detailed profiling and optimization can wait, enabling quick cycle times for isolating and solving performance issues cannot. Investing in observability tools and performance engineering processes will be a fundamental key to avoid non-productive performance anxiety.
- Teams and leaders need to understand the benefits of optimizing for concerns that are complex to mitigate (e.g., cycle time) rather than concerns that are simpler to mitigate (e.g., network latency).
- Strive for increased parity across technical environments. When the various environments used to develop and test software lack uniformity, the process for profiling and optimizing performance

improvements becomes increasingly difficult (e.g., It's hard to predict the efficacy of a driving technique in a Ferrari by testing it in a Honda Civic).

• Understand how to quantify the value of performance across multiple contexts. Leaders and practitioners in online retail and media spaces are deeply versed in how milliseconds of performance improvements can improve revenue generation by millions of dollars. Outside of these industries, however, many firms lack any ability to quantify the value of improved versus degraded performance. Without a basic understanding of how performance translates to enterprise value, your teams will be left to engage in battles of dramatic speculation that often lack the grounding and sophistication necessary to make informed decisions that are optimized for the most valuable outcome.

Increased Risk to Quality Issues

Risk: More moving parts means more things to break. This is a fundamental truth of engineering, and it is not our contention that increasing the usage of decoupled modules will not have any impact on your ability to ensure quality in the delivery of your digital products.

Signs to Look For: You'll know this risk has materialized or is looming when:

• Your teams are overly reliant on manual testing practices and lack modern standards and sufficient tools for managing software quality (e.g., defect tracking software is the bare minimum and can't be the sole tooling investment for your teams to ensure quality).
• QA cycles and disciplines are segmented in a silo separated from software development and engineering.
• No reliable and automated means of tracking basic QA metrics exists, including QA cycle times, defect escape rates, and mean time to recovery.

- Experiments run on without end, leading to them being considered long-term solutions. This creates quality issues as POCs (proofs of concept) are not engineered for industrial use.
- DevOps and CI/CD are exclusively focused on deployment automation rather than the full set of tasks to take a candidate release from one environment to the next.

Mitigation Strategy: Ensure teams are supplied with the appropriate guideposts and tools that will help them shift left in their approach to quality engineering:

- Institutionalize an approach to ensuring quality that includes automated metric trend reporting, automated static-analysis and mitigation tooling, canary testing in production with controlled audiences, and treating testing automation on the same plane as infrastructure and deployment automation.
- Ritualize the process of asking teams to compress the timeline, risk, and scale of experiments. Work with teams to investigate the possibilities of testing with a smaller feature set, smaller audience group, smaller target of applicability, or any other method they can think of to shrink the timeline and risk of an experiment.

Increased Operational Complexity

Risk: More moving parts, "black boxes" of opaque functionality, and greater interdependency will inevitably make your enterprise more complex to operate.

Signs to Look For: You'll know this risk is bound to materialize when:

- Documentation is scarce and automated onboarding tools for API consumers are not provisioned.

- Your teams must routinely engage in unplanned work for security, performance, or quality incidents.
- Your organization has not formalized an approach for managing and communicating changes to your APIs.

Mitigation Strategy: Ensure teams are familiar with and have the enterprise support to:

- Be disciplined in your commitment to require teams that make APIs to assume that the APIs will be consumed by external parties at some point in their life span.
- Utilize the practices from performance ("prepare early and optimize late") and quality management ("shift left") to enable teams with a smooth path to isolate and repair problems that arose from dependencies that are not well understood.
- Establish a set of shared principles and practices for managing and communicating changes to your APIs.

Misapplying the MVP Concept

Risk: Throughout this book, we've spoken to the concepts of running market-facing trials and small experiments with low risk and expenditure. While many teams and organizations have adopted Lean development practices and the embedded concept of an MVP, not every team or leader fully understands the intended meaning and application of the MVP concept.

Introduced by Frank Robinson in 2001 and later popularized by Eric Ries in *Lean Startup*, the MVP has become a foundational concept to enterprises working on software projects around the globe.

While most everyone understands "minimum," not all teams are aligned on the meaning of "viable" or "product" in this context. The MVP concept was intended to be defined as the version of a new product that allows teams to gather the maximum amount of validated customer feedback with minimal effort. It is not about creating the product with the least number of features necessary for a public launch, but rather a tool for testing hypotheses and discovering what will meet customers' needs.

Signs to Look For: You'll know this risk has materialized when your teams exhibit any of the following behaviors:

- Teams scope experiments around a product concept that has everything required for a commercial launch.
- Teams look to enable the full set of capabilities and controls required for scaled usage and edge case scenarios.
- Teams cannot express the basic consumer need or pain point that they're trying to validate.
- Teams fail to consider that experiments must be iterative to yield useful feedback.

When looking at the above listing of behaviors, pay close attention to the last example regarding the need for iteration. Whether your teams will need to build upon the learnings from a single trial or rework the assumptions and offering to find sufficient market fit, it will almost always be necessary for teams to perform several variations of an experiment to deliver the "maximum amount of validated customer feedback with minimal effort."

Mitigation Strategy: Ensure teams are supplied with the guideposts and support that will help them:

- When teams struggle with finding the right balance between "minimum" and "viable," remind them of the intended goal and that the important thing is to focus on the principles of customer satisfaction, continuous improvement, and simplicity.
- Remind teams up front that experiments are serial in nature and that enabling their trial concepts to be extensible via modularity is required to capture the intended learnings of the experiment.

Cannibalizing Existing Revenue

Risk: A consequence of enabling new digital channels of value consumption for your consumers is that these new channels can sometimes be competitive with existing channels of value consumption that already generate revenue for your enterprise. When considering experiments and offerings that might overlap with existing products and services, it is critical that your product teams have a nuanced understanding of financial details of the existing revenue streams (e.g., the amounts and trends of existing revenue streams, the operating margins of existing offerings, the likelihood of disruption to these existing revenue streams, etc.).

Signs to Look For: You'll know this risk is in the process of manifesting when:

- Digital product teams are experimenting with or launching offerings that have a high degree of overlap in the value that other enterprise products and services already supply.
- Product development teams fail to evaluate how new digital offerings will lead to revenue growth for any existing offerings.
- Product development teams fail to evaluate how new digital offerings can be positioned as extensions and add-ons to existing offerings.
- Product development work in the software engineering lane is segmented from or independent of packaging and go-to-market strategy.

Mitigation Strategy: Ensure teams are supplied with the tools and techniques to understand value dynamics:

- Utilize value exchange mapping techniques (detailed in Chapter 5) to understand not only the opportunities of unbundled offerings but also the possible competitive positions that your new offerings might take against your existing offerings.

- Require teams to consider how an external product would generate recurring revenue via a packaging strategy before formalizing
on an externalized interface design.

Technology-Centered Transformation

Risk: When technology teams charter and run business transformation initiatives, the tendency is for the objectives of those initiatives to be framed as
technology-specific objectives rather than business objectives.

Signs to Look For: You'll know this risk area needs attention when:

- Initiative objectives are framed in technology-centric outcomes
rather than business-centric outcomes (e.g., "Complete a shift
to cloud-based infrastructure" rather than "Measurably increase
speed to market of digital solutions by leveraging cloud-based
infrastructure").
- Delivery teams cite low business team participation and engagement in initiatives.
- Business and finance teams view the initiative as a technology-
driven program.
- Teams spend inordinate amounts of time debating on low-
value topics like protocol wars (e.g., GraphQL versus REST) at
the expense of fully understanding how to reshape the process
and operating models that undergird the mission-critical value
streams.

Mitigation Strategy: Ensure teams are supplied with the tools and techniques to:

- Ground objectives in measurable outcomes that are specifically
relevant to business leadership inclusive of sales, finance, marketing, etc.

- Offer training programs and educational reimbursement programs to build digital business skills along with basic API literacy.
- Frame APIs as products regardless of any immediate plans for external consumption.
- Help teams understand that products—units or vehicles of value delivery from a producer to a consumer—are not the exclusive domain of the product department or organizational unit (e.g., Is an employee portal or intranet a product? Would it be a bad thing if it were treated like one? Would it be a good thing if it was not?) and that product methods and mindsets need to be applied to give an appropriate level of stewardship and support to company assets.
- Keep teams focused on the concept that group collaboration time must be heavily focused on business and operating model evolution and not on ideological wars that only concern a small segment of the teams.
- Frame and ground transformation programs in the context of business and financial needs rather than technology outcomes. (Dr. Mik Kersten's book *Project to Product* is an excellent resource to help people and teams approach and understand this topic.)

Misaligned Talent Model and Processes

Risk: Traditional talent recruiting and development models rightly place an emphasis on skills that are perceived as "core" to a specific role. As explained in Chapter 5, developing fluency in statistical analysis and tools will be necessary to keep the cost of experimentation low.

Signs to Look For: You'll know this risk has materialized when:

- Teams report on KPIs with an over-reliance on proxy metrics and singular numbers that don't convey context (trends, percentages, inverse/direct correlations, averages rather than medians, etc.).

- Teams habitually align behaviors to localized goals at the expense of enterprise goals.

Mitigation Strategy: Ensure teams are supplied with the tools and techniques to recruit and develop the skills needed for scaled unbundling:

- Develop job descriptions that incorporate "m-shaped" profiles, where contributors are expected to have some proficiency in, and appreciation for, tasks and processes that are utilized by teams that they will be collaborating with.
- Offer training programs and educational reimbursement programs to build data visualization skills along with statistical literacy.
- Commit to using balanced scorecards, shared goals, and other talent management techniques that require collaboration and shared decision-making to achieve enterprise-level outcomes.

Losing Discipline in Times of Compression

Risk: In Chapter 6, we spoke at length regarding enterprise behaviors in times of disruption and compression. While "belt-tightening" mindsets are not fully avoidable given the nature of financial viability, it is advisable to arm yourself with tools and tactics to mitigate the impacts of organizational compression, especially in the areas where financial compression tactics are not aligned with preservation of value creation.

Signs to Look For: You'll know this risk will soon materialize when:

- Economic factors align to drive significant cutbacks across an industry or geographic segment.
- Technology teams align to a platform model before business teams see the platform as a core component to the enterprise business model.

- Teams are short-lived constructs that serve a project charter rather than a product charter.

Mitigation Strategy: Ensure teams and leaders are familiar with and aligned to:

- The S-curve model of business management to allow for a measured and moderated conversation on targeted cutbacks paired with reinvestment on future horizons.
- Not formalizing platform teams in advance of business understanding of the concept and acceptance of the offering as core to the enterprise business model.
- Product-based finance models that include carve-outs to manage cross-cutting concerns like performance, quality, security, automation, and debt management.

Choosing the Wrong Interface to Control

Risk: A precept of how modularity and optionality work together to deliver scaled value opportunities is that you must choose where interfaces should lie along a value stream of activities, which interfaces you'll want to tightly control access to, and which interfaces you'll want to encourage engagement with. This concept is explained in depth in Chapter 3 and references the work of Dr. Carliss Baldwin when it explains that controlling the interfaces to value rather than just the systems that deliver value is the better strategy.

Signs to Look For: You'll know this risk will eventually materialize when:

- Your teams don't have a process for understanding and evaluating how and when consumer value is added and harvested in your value streams.
- Your enterprise has an extreme approach that either excludes all forms of partner-based delivery (a fully closed ecosystem) or has

a Wild West approach to partner-based delivery (a fully open ecosystem with no methods for generating revenue via partner engagement).

Mitigation Strategy: Ensure teams have support to:

- Utilize value exchange mapping techniques (detailed in Chapter 5) to understand where value is harvested by your firm, the partners you work with, and the end consumers.
- Develop and evolve a rubric for both understanding your firm's competencies (e.g., Are we qualified and able to market this unbundled offering to its likely consumers?) and judging the value at stake with a candidate offering.

Pervasive Use of Performative Behaviors (AKA: Optionality Theater)

Risk: All corporate initiatives are subject to the risks associated with performative compliance. Lean, Agile, DevOps, and API transformations are no exception to this rule. If your enterprise engages in an unbundling initiative or a digital transformation that is driven in part by APIs, at least some of your teams and leaders will engage in "optionality theater" to appear compliant with directives from enterprise leaders.

Signs to Look For: You'll know this risk will materialize soon when:

- Reward systems are indexed exclusively to shallow proxy metrics (e.g., number of APIs created, number of experiments executed, etc.) rather than business outcomes.
- You hear teams defend poor judgment, lack of critical thinking, and cutting corners that impact downstream teams by referring to hard rules that don't offer insight into applying them with a smart mindset.

Mitigation Strategy: Ensure teams are supplied with the tools and techniques to:

- Commit to using balanced scorecards, shared goals, and other talent management techniques that require collaboration and shared decision-making to achieve enterprise-level outcomes.
- Identify and root out processes where decision rights are granted to people and teams that don't bear the consequences of those decisions (e.g., decision-makers must have "skin in the game" for the impacts of their choices).

12

Embracing Uncertainty

Throughout this book, we've focused our attention on unpacking the events of the past to make sense of the present. We did this with an aim to help you prepare for the future. Despite our central thesis that the future is inherently unpredictable, we do want to take a moment and look at some real-time events, see how APIs are driving them, and think about what options might be interesting to create and conserve.

The Rise of Generative AI

The hottest trend that has captivated the world as we write this book is the rise of ChatGPT and, more generically, the power of generative AI. While we're still seeing the potential of AI unfold across nearly every industry and labor pool, in the context of this book, it is interesting to note that much of the wildfire spread and impact of ChatGPT can be, unsurprisingly, traced to API-centered factors.

- The standards-based API interface of OpenAI has made the costs of coordination and integration with the capabilities of ChatGPT so low that almost every software producing company (except for the ones competing for AI supremacy) have already rolled

out new features in their own offerings powered by OpenAI and
other providers' large language models (LLMs).

- The companies who've moved the fastest to integrate generative
AI capabilities have been able to do so in part because much of
the consuming applications themselves were already unbundled
into segmented modules that communicate through APIs.

Given the wide acceptance of standards-based, API-enabled value
exchange, it's not surprising that the world has witnessed a flood of other
AI-based tools over the last eighteen months. As these tools became ready
for scaled usage, we've seen who was ready to quickly consume the AI capabilities into their offerings because their digital offerings were already built
to consume and integrate external services. We have also seen how many
organizations were left flat-footed and unable to evolve and exploit the fastest adoption curve the world has ever seen because their software offerings
lacked the modularity necessary to integrate a host of external services at a
low cost.

A somewhat hidden factor that both drives and feeds off the rise of
abstract services like generative AI is the long-running trend where the
increasing efficiency of value exchanges causes channel migration and organizational transformation.

A defining factor of commerce and business shifting to online channels is how digital transactions lower the coordination cost of interactions.
A major reason businesses of all types have invested first in the web, then
in mobile, and now in APIs is that these technologies lower coordination
costs and increase the efficiency of value exchange. Digital channels have a
price advantage compared to physical channels, which carry all sorts of physical world costs associated with pesky and unpredictable humans. As API
proliferation and machine-to-machine/bot-to-bot interactions become the
prevalent means of value exchange, we'll begin to see a host of other behavior
changes take effect.

Just like we explained in Chapter 5, where lowering the cost of running
experiments will cause a rise in demand for experiments, we're likely to see a
plethora of behavior changes for enterprises when coordination costs fall pre-

cipitously. Perhaps the most far-reaching change will come in how enterprises approach fundamental execution questions like buy versus build. When the risk and cost of outsourcing capabilities to external specialty firms significantly falls, leasing market-proven capabilities from a specialist will become increasingly compelling when compared to keeping capabilities in-house.

The proliferation of hyper-specialized offerings (small firms with offerings that are both highly targeted and abstract) is poised to continue its acceleration while simultaneously making larger firms more efficient and productive. Where less than a few years ago, firms like Twilio or BazaarVoice were rare and unproven, today the launching of new specialized SaaS companies is an everyday occurrence.

APIs are at the heart of this change as their nature (standards-based interaction models that have a low, one-time, fixed cost of provisioning for execution combined with extremely low variable cost of execution) is significantly responsible for driving the continued decrease in the cost of multiparty interactions.

The broad adoption of API-based integration models by development communities has democratized an ever-expanding range of digital capabilities. What started out as basic computing infrastructure and content services has advanced through telephony automation, payments, and audio processing and brought other highly complex concepts like software-driven networking or generative AI within the reach of small and medium businesses.

Not only is it simpler than ever to provision and use distributed capabilities, but information hiding via modularity has also made it possible for firms to "not care" about the messy details of fulfillment (e.g., Do you really need to know how Twilio manages to deliver messages to phones on any network, anywhere in the world?).

One potential future implication of the fall in interaction costs is that large sectors of the global economy will depend upon increasingly complex networks of decoupled providers. A natural outcome of this increased dependency is that the need to increase service robustness and fault-tolerant services will increase because the amount of value dependent upon these efficient exchanges will be "too big to fail." This increased need for reliability may cause the emergence of a new type of provider—a meta-aggregator that manages and routes traffic to the most efficient source of fulfillment for a range of capabilities.

These types of meta providers already exist in a limited fashion. Multi-CDN providers, for example, aggregate individual CDN providers (content delivery networks like Akamai, Fastly, and others) and deliver a higher level of reliability to enterprises that need efficient forms of content delivery.

As generative AI has been adopted by organizations around the world, we've begun to see novel applications where AI is being used to accelerate and improve software development processes. This specific capability will act as a flywheel and accelerate the maturation of generative AI capabilities. While it's not possible to predict every outcome that is on the horizon, one likely outcome lies in the as-of-yet unfulfilled dreams of the inventor of the World Wide Web—Sir Tim Berners-Lee.

In 1999, Sir Tim Berners-Lee, one of *Time Magazine*'s one hundred most important people of the twentieth century, and one of only six members of the World Wide Web Hall of Fame, coined the term "the semantic web" and expressed a vision for how machines would be able to talk to other machines, stating:

> I have a dream for the Web [where computers] become capable of analyzing all the data on the Web—the content, links, and transactions between people and computers. A "Semantic Web," which makes this possible, has yet to emerge, but when it does, the day-to-day mechanisms of trade, bureaucracy and our daily lives will be handled by machines talking to machines. The "intelligent agents" people have touted for ages will finally materialize.[1]

While there has been some progress to bring this vision to reality, generative AI looks like it will be the key that unlocks this capability because LLMs like those provided by OpenAI, Google, Anthropic, and other tools are the "intelligent agents" Berners-Lee referred to. In the same way IaaS capabilities unlocked a new level of optionality (explained in Chapter 5), generative AI tools will be the catalyst that allows society to tackle or bypass most, if not all, of the major obstacles to realization.

Automated reasoning systems like ChatGPT can finally deliver on the promise of the semantic web because LLMs can automate the reasoning processes that, until now, were only doable by humans with the capacity to apply reason in a vague space. Because machine learning and LLM tools have the capability of automating tedious work, generative AI will unlock the capability to make every API-based service "self-describing." This one spark will accelerate digital connectivity by overcoming challenges that have seemed insurmountable for the last twenty years (e.g., vastness, vagueness, uncertainty, inconsistency, deceit, etc.). For APIs, this means coordination costs will drop again as APIs become self-describing once LLM agents are pointed toward them (making integration and consumption of digital capabilities even easier than they are today).

As the cost of exchange drops, the volume of demand and consumption of hyper-specialized offerings will continue to rise, making the need for meta-aggregators more likely while also making them more financially viable. One potential outcome of this trend could be that the aggregators evolve into abstract hubs of redundant capabilities designed to ensure the highest possible levels of availability. Imagine a service that allows you to utilize Microsoft Azure for a set of workloads and seamlessly switches that workload to AWS, RedShift, Google Cloud, Salesforce, or any other emergent provider if Azure is experiencing latency or some form of downtime. Now take that idea one step further and imagine a service that aggregates and coordinates multiple types of packaged capabilities from multiple providers, allowing the consumer to only pay for the ones they use and always receiving the service from the most efficient and reliable provider.

When taking the above possible futures into a single context, a new world of possibility emerges, where multiple types of generative AI can be strung together (by an AI agent fluent with APIs) to enable chat-based capabilities for highly complex macro tasks that can be invoked by ubiquitous and ambient interfaces. "Hey, Siri. Make me a website to help me market and sell my book titled *Unbundling the Enterprise.*"

While the prognostications above may seem far-fetched in terms of scope or time horizons, a major takeaway from this book is intended to help you see the future in terms of possibility. A possibility that invites exploration into a set of potential options. Your potential portfolio of potential options stands to generate large returns if you've deliberately aligned your financial and technical processes to support generating optionality. The questions to ask yourself and your enterprise are:

1. Given the radical change we are all about to experience with the emergence of generative AI, have we invested in generating our own OOOps moments?
2. Have we already taken the step of unbundling and modularizing our capabilities through API-led decomposition (an architectural pattern for separating functional capabilities across distinct layers of APIs that often call each other in sequence)? When our capabilities are granular, unbundled, and addressable via standardized interfaces, our options can be generated and conserved prior to the future fully materializing. The choice we make today leaves open the possibility for us to maximize our chances for big returns.
3. Have we already taken the step of mapping our ecosystem including how value is exchanged across it? When our ecosystem is mapped and familiar to our delivery teams, our use of resources can be optimized to focus on options that might be valuable to entities that are in our ecosystem (e.g., our customers and partners). The choice we make today sets us up to be a proactive solver of problems with the communities we engage with.
4. Have we already taken the step of paving and optimizing our feedback loops? When our ability to iteratively learn and adapt is optimized for low-cost trials, we can rapidly focus our efforts behind options that show the promise of having a path to serial growth through ecosystem adoption.

The AI revolution we are now living through has many parallels to the Industrial Revolution that we can learn from. During the first Industrial Revolution, steam power shifted the manufacturing paradigm, but many constraints remained. When the new electrically driven paradigm accelerated, it wasn't through the new power source—electricity—alone. It was through a combination of electricity and future optionality. Optionality came in the form of interchangeable parts (which modularized products) and the assembly line (which modularized production).

Prepare Early, Decide Late

We began Chapter 1 of this book with Thomas Edison's moment of triumph as he switched on a light bulb in 1882, illuminating not only his present day but the likely future paths of innovation as well. Making that light spread and be accessible to populations all over the world took imagination, many more innovations, and a healthy dose of modularity to walk down that future path to an electrified and illuminated society.

In the digital world we all inhabit today, our path to the future is somehow both hidden in shadow and illuminated at the same time. The shadow is the uncertain future, and the illumination is the methodology to systematically pull the undiscovered and confusing future into the well-understood present—prepare early by unbundling your enterprise with the three OOOps methods so you can decide late as the future unfolds and reveals itself. Unbundling your business capabilities to create more convex options can be your enterprise's path to digital prosperity, even if you can no longer tell if it was by accident, by design, or, perhaps, both.

Conclusion

━━━━

Set Sail to the Land of a Thousand Shovels

N ow that we've reached the end of this book, we hope you've seen and understand that the fastest path to buried treasure in our increasingly digital world isn't with a map where a single X marks the spot. Our intention has not been to rip the map out of your hand, but instead to give you a new set of tools (the three OOOps methods) infinitely more valuable than a single map that may or may not actually lead to a single treasure.

OPtionality

OPportunities

OPtimization

FIGURE C.1: The Three OOOps Methods

When used in concert, these three methods will help you simultaneously lower your risk while raising your potential rewards. By using the first OOOps method (create optionality through unbundled APIs), you'll not only be able to weather unforeseen disruptions, you'll also be able to afford "a thousand shovels" primed to find the winning options by lowering the cost to bundle and unbundle your offerings until new futures reveal themselves. The second method (identify opportunities through value dynamics) will help you navigate the mysteries of the unknown future and draw you to the islands where the treasures are not buried too deeply. The third method (drive optimization through feedback loops) works symbiotically with the first two methods and enables you to spread your low-cost drones far and wide to dig a thousand holes at once.

The digital paradigm is still being established today in a way that closely mirrors the electrical transformation that emerged more than a century ago. Software, hardware, and data abound, but the methods of leveraging them at scale are still being figured out. In this book, we have explored the winning methods and strategies of established global enterprises across a variety of industries. In doing so, we uncovered the principles and practices that hold the key to unlock sustainable digital success.

There are many familiar attributes and perspectives at leading digital companies. They have courageous leaders who are willing to take short-term pain for long-term gain. They invest in acquiring skills and establishing foundational competencies. They view their business from their customers' perspective and align their organizations accordingly. In our research for this book, we wanted to take a closer look at the all-too-often overlooked attribute these organizations have in common: the way they have structured their businesses around unbundled digital capabilities.

Throughout *Unbundling the Enterprise*, we have shown how digital pirates utilized this unbundling approach to drive optionality in their organizations, creating conditions for happy accidents they used to disrupt industries and enter new markets. Amazon Web Services was spawned from existing capabilities that Amazon composed into a new service offering. The Google Maps API was unbundled from the web app to open new channels and drive exponential growth and market dominance. Facebook's unbundling of its core capabilities into a developer platform led to its viral spread across the web and set the table for its ad revenue–driven business model. These digital pirates have set the template for the twenty-first century enterprise.

When looking at the dramatic successes of the digital pirates, we ask you to remember that the digital economy has open borders. It is not for the original digital pirates alone. We have seen how Coca-Cola used API-enabled capabilities to get customer input on product innovation while establishing a new direct customer channel. We learned how Best Buy used a digital platform foundation to create cross-functional service offerings that benefited its retailers, its repair unit, and its customers. We saw how Cox Automotive leveraged the core competencies of its multiple business lines to digitally transform its automotive ecosystem. In each of these examples, the company executed a deliberate strategy of increasing optionality, then yielded happy accidents as a result.

Before the year 2000, no business leader ever said, "We need an API to take our business to the next level." That changed when Jeff Bezos saw that APIs represented the next evolutionary stage of how innumerable types of value would be exchanged between organizations. Over the last two decades, global society has witnessed just how prescient Bezos was when he forced Amazon to adapt to the relentless force that has been driving business since the dawn of the Industrial Revolution. This force unfolds over time, slowly at first and accelerating until it ultimately drives all exchanges of value to the available channel of highest efficiency.

The force, rooted in economic scarcity and human competitiveness, is unyielding. It drives the evolution of every business process to new levels of efficiency regardless of any sentimental attachment to that which is familiar or comforting. Both the owners and participants of established processes and channels almost always resist the force despite all historical evidence that their best move is, like a person who fell out of the boat in the middle of a rapid river, to swim with the current of change.

When a new, more efficient mode of commercial exchange becomes possible, not only do businesses around the world get pulled downstream by the current of higher efficiency, but these same organizations see the growth rate of these new types of exchanges ramp at a pace that was previously unfathomable. This new mode, powered by a reduction in overall coordination costs, is only accelerating as generative AI catalyzes and increases the shift in coordination costs from repetitive variable costs that are incurred with every exchange of value to costs that are mostly fixed costs constrained to a single instance when a digital service is provisioned for self-service consumption. You don't need an advanced degree in economics or a background in history of commerce technology to see the river and its current, because we are all living in it right now.

As a result of this migration to higher efficiency, concepts that were once part of the fabric of our everyday lives effectively get labeled obsolete as they are replaced by new, more efficient ideas.

- Retail enterprises have, in recent years, felt the impact of the current as the concepts that are associated with purchasing both everyday and luxury items have been completely upended. Twenty years ago, online commerce was a niche concept, but in 2023, the efficiency and convenience of online shopping is now the dominant form of value exchange in retail, specifically because it is more efficient for all parties involved.
- Media organizations from news to entertainment are experiencing turbulence and volatility around the globe as information dissemination has evolved to the point where value is more closely aligned with the delivery of content you find comfort in rather than information that is grounded in objective truth. Fixed forms of media that are tied to physical objects and locations have been whipsawed for the last two decades, leaving new entrants to split the pie of media revenue with the players who've adapted their economic and delivery models to one that embraces digital optionality based in APIs.
- Financial service firms have begun to react to the inroads carved out by the wave of highly specialized fintech offerings from both startups and aggressive digital pirates who ground their consumer-friendly offerings in API services and mobile user engagement.
- Firms that manufacture and sell consumer goods that range from soft goods to durables are beginning to imbue their offerings and distribution strategies with loosely coupled APIs to find new

ways to grow revenue from engaging and satisfying consumers while simultaneously lowering costs and increasing flexibility.

- Transportation and hospitality are increasing their investments in APIs to drive innovation and enhance consumer experiences. Whether it's opening to affiliates and aggregators or enabling a new level of personalization and customization, the choice between potential revenue growth on one side and the slow creep of irrelevance on the other has forced these industries to see themselves as inextricably tied to digital strategies that center around API offerings.
- The explosion of healthcare APIs keeps accelerating as medical ecosystem players leverage APIs for everything from monitoring patient data to accepting payments and even the tedious task of multiparty calendaring.

The forces that push and pull the global marketplace are not limited to the above industries. Firms within energy production and distribution, the public sector, and even space exploration are all reacting to the swift current that simultaneously rewards modularity and punishes rigidity.

Before the year 2000, the business necessity of embracing the World Wide Web wasn't as clear and concrete as it is today. In 2024, the naysayers on this topic have, for all intents and purposes, gone silent. That same process of pivoting to a new set of rules for value exchange is not only recurring right now but also happening beneath the notice of many leaders and firms who remain blissfully unaware that API traffic is eating the internet at a pace that keeps accelerating (reported by Akamai to be at 83% of all internet traffic in 2018).[1]

The changes in how parties complete an exchange of value from specific physical spaces and low-efficiency processes to virtual channels with more efficient processes has defined the evolution of commerce since the dawn of the Industrial Revolution (shown in Figure C.2). In the last twenty years, the pervasive success of the World Wide Web has exponentially accelerated this migration of where and how value is exchanged. This acceleration has been so palpable that the current shared experience we are all living in makes it feel like we are not only living through the rapids of the river, but that we are approaching and about to go over the steep waterfall that will leave behind every other mode of exchange to the unattractive category of obsolescence.

API-based consumption has exceeded every other previous mode of consumption in lowering coordination costs and raising exchange efficiency. In most scenarios, API-based consumption reduces dependencies, handoffs, and other unpredictable sources of delay and error.

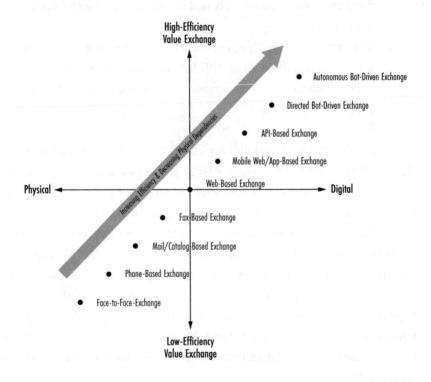

FIGURE C.2: Systematically Building Optionality

As AI advances make self-describing services and autonomous agents jump off the page of science fiction to join real people in the real world, we stand at a unique point in time. Where every evolutionary step in the past has yielded a supplanting of an old channel with the dominance of a new one, bots and agents aren't likely to leave API channels behind. Rather, the intelligent and autonomous algorithms of the future will further accelerate the amount of traffic and activity channeled through APIs, specifically because the provided API interfaces are already optimized for machine-driven consumption.

The captains of industry have historically steered their ships toward known markets and opportunities since the dawn of the Industrial Revolution. A handful of digital pirates have successfully rewritten the rules of finance and ROI by stumbling into opportunities they could not have foreseen.

Making Your Own Luck

When you close this book, we don't want you to just put it on the shelf. We want you to take what you've learned and put it into action. By adopting the "new math" of successful digital companies, you can better incentivize and align around optionality at your organization. Whether you are a digital novice or an experienced API aficionado, you can use value dynamics to better understand your current business model and your competitive landscape and assess new opportunities for digital innovation. To better understand where to place your bets, you can establish the right feedback loops between your customers, your products, and the constituents in your ecosystem. By using these techniques, you can make sure the happy accidents you experience won't just be paint smudges you turn into birds or happy little trees. Your happy accidents will be the financial options you choose to exercise opportunistically when your capabilities and market conditions line up.

The digital economy moves quickly. Real-time connectivity between companies is driving coordination costs lower and lower. But the cost of doing nothing has never been higher. Companies that are down the path with APIs and optionality are already operating in the frame of digital ecosystems. In that context, they drive even more optionality by offering their own unbundled capabilities to (and leveraging API-enabled products from) third parties. These are the conditions that will allow companies to quickly adopt new innovations around AI and the next wave of stunning innovations made possible because of AI. That agility, born out of modularity, will be existential in short order. We've all lived through the times where well-established companies and even industries have seen their offerings repackaged and commoditized by digital pirates in ways that make old models wither and fade into irrelevance— and the forces that instigated these changes are only speeding up.

Our aim in writing this book has been to equip leaders and practitioners at enterprises around the world with the insight and understanding necessary to seek out and capture these unpredictable treasures. The tools and the rules to being a relevant player in the global economy are changing faster than ever. Our hope, now that this work is completed, is that our readers see that you don't need a future-seeing visionary to help you unearth the next big digital opportunity. Rather, it is just the opposite. The path to uncapped future gains starts with acknowledgment of lack of fortune-telling capabilities and the courage to invest in uncertain futures where the most modular enterprises have the upper hand.

With the global tumult of economic earthquakes (e.g., the arrival of the modern web, the mobile boom, the COVID-19 pandemic, the rise of generative AI, the unpredictable tastes of younger consumers, etc.), it has never been so clear: the most valuable treasures out there are the ones you don't yet know to look for.

Bibliography

Akamai. "Retail Attacks and API Traffic." [*State of the Internet*] / Security 5, no. 2. (February 2019). https://www.akamai.com/site/it/documents/state-of-the-internet/state-of-the-internet-security -retail-attacks-and-api-traffic-report-2019.pdf.

"Amazon Web Services - Adam Selipsky at USI," YouTube video, 47:01, posted by USI Events, posted on September 6 2013. https://www.youtube.com/watch?v=6PiyzyWXiIk&t=300s.

"Amazon Web Services Launches." Amazon press release. March 14, 2006. https://press.aboutamazon.com/2006/3/amazon-web-services-launches.

Andreessen, Marc. "Yo." Genius.com. Accessed March 8, 2024. https://genius.com/Marc-andreessen -yo-annotated.

Andrzejek, David. "Becoming a Fintech: Capital One's Move From Mainframes to the Cloud." *CIO*, May 19, 2023. https://www.cio.com/article/350288/becoming-a-fintech-capital-ones-move -from-mainframes-to-the-cloud.html.

Appleyard, Bryan. "Books That Helped to Change The World." *The Sunday Times*. July 19, 2009. https://www.thetimes.co.uk/article/books-that-helped-to-change-the-world-qbhxgvg2kwh.

Arrington, Michael. "Facebook Launches Facebook Platform; They are the Anti-MySpace." *TechCrunch*. May 24, 2007. https://TechCrunch.com/2007/05/24/facebook-launches-facebook -platform-they-are-the-anti-myspace/.

Arrington, Michael. "Facebook to Release a 'Like' Button for the Whole Darn Internet." *TechCrunch*. March 25, 2010. https://TechCrunch.com/2010/03/25/facebook-to-release-a-like-button-for -the-whole-darn-internet/.

Associated Press, The. "Number of Active Users at Facebook Over the Years." Yahoo News. May 1, 2013. https://news.yahoo.com/number-active-users-facebook-over-230449748.html.

"A Transformational Legacy." UCLA website. Accessed on March 8, 2024. https://www.anderson .ucla.edu/about/our-history.

"Auto Innovators: New Data on Auto Industry's Economic Impact." Alliance for Automotive Inno-vation press release. November 30, 2022. https://www.autosinnovate.org/posts/press-release/ new-data-on-economic-impact.

Baldwin, Carliss Y., and Kim B. Clark. *Design Rules: The Power of Mudlarity*. Cambridge, MA: MIT Press, 2000.

Baldwin, Carliss Y., and C. Jason Woodard. "The Architecture of Platforms: A Unified View." *Social Science Research Network*, January 1, 2008. https://doi.org/10.2139/ssrn.1265155.

Barr, Jeff. "We Build Muck, So You Don't Have To." AWS News (blog). September 27, 2006. https://aws.amazon.com/blogs/aws/we_build_muck_s/.

Bell, Melissa. "Google Engineer Steve Yegge Has His Jerry Maguire Moment." *The Washington Post*. October 14, 2011. https://www.washingtonpost.com/blogs/blogpost/post/google-engineer -steve-yegge-has-his-jerry-maguire-moment/2011/10/13/gIQATU1hkL_blog.html.

Benzell, Seth G., Jonathan Hersh, and Marshall W. Van Alstyne. "How APIs Create Growth by Inverting the Firm." *Social Science Research Network*. September 30, 2022. https://papers.ssrn.com/sol3/papers.cfm?abstract_id=3432591.

Berners-Lee, Tim. *Weaving the Web: The Original Design and Ultimate Destiny of the World Wide Web*. New York: HarperOne, 1999.

Best Buy. *Best Buy Co., Inc.* Fiscal 2000 Annual Report. 2000. https://www.annualreports.com/HostedData/AnnualReportArchive/b/NYSE_BBY_2000.pdf.

"Business Model Canvas." Strategyzer (website). February 26, 2024. https://www.strategyzer.com/library/the-business-model-canvas.

Carlier, Mathilde. "U.S. New and Used Car Sales 2010-2022." Statista (website). August 29, 2023. https://www.statista.com/statistics/183713/value-of-us-passenger-cas-sales-and-leases-since-1990/#:~:text=Sales%20of%20used%20light%20vehicles,and%20automobiles%20were%20sold%20here.

Castle, Scott. "Who Are Knowledge Workers and How Do We Enable Them?" *Forbes*. December 1, 2021. https://www.forbes.com/sites/sisense/2021/12/01/who-are-knowledge-workers-and.-how-do-we-enable-them/?sh=19be99296018.

Christensen, Clayton M. *The Innovator's Dilemma: When New Technologies Cause Great Firms to Fail*. Boston, MA: Harvard Business School Press, 1997.

Christensen, Clayton M., and Andy Jassy. "60. Overcoming the Capitalist's Dilemma, with Andy Jassy, CEO of Amazon Web Services." The Disruptive Voice podcast, 53:04. September 1, 2020. https://thedisruptivevoice.libsyn.com/60-overcoming-the-capitalists-dilemma-with-andy-jassy-ceo-of-amazon-web-services.

Collins, Jim. "Return on Luck." JimCollins.com. Accessed on March 8, 2024. https://www.jimcollins.com/concepts/return-on-luck.html.

Collins, Jim, and Morten T. Hansen. "How to Manage Through Chaos." JimCollins.com. October 2011. https://www.jimcollins.com/article_topics/articles/how-to-manage-through-chaos.html#articletop.

Conway, Melvin E. "How Do Committees Invent." *Datamation*. April 1968. https://web.archive.org/web/20190919111512/http://melconway.com/Home/Committees_Paper.html.

Crosby, Jackie. "One Man's Force of Will Built a Retailing Empire." *StarTribune*. May 19, 2012. https://www.startribune.com/one-man-s-force-of-will-built-a-retailing-empire/152098405/.

Curry, David. "Slack Revenue and Usage Statistics (2024)." Business of Apps (website). January 15, 2024. https://www.businessofapps.com/data/slack-statistics/.

DevExchange, Capital One. "Behind the Scenes at Capital One DevExchange—Capital One Tech—Medium." Medium. February 28, 2020. https://medium.com/capital-one-tech/behind-the-scenes-at-capital-one-devexchange-2b0702f2399b.

Dixon, Stacy Jo. "Annual Revenue and Net Income Generated by Meta Platforms from 2007 to 2023." Statista (website). March 4, 2024. https://www.statista.com/statistics/277229/facebooks-annual-revenue-and-net-income/.

Doyle, Noah. "Official Google Maps API Blog: Google Maps for Enterprise." Google Maps API (blog), June 14, 2006. https://googlemapsapi.blogspot.com/2006/06/google-maps-for-enterprise.html.

Drucker, Peter F. "The Theory of the Business." *Harvard Business Review*. September-October 1994. https://hbr.org/1994/09/the-theory-of-the-business.

"Facebook Reports Fourth Quarter and Full Year 2019 Results." Meta Investor Relations (website). January 29, 2020. https://investor.fb.com/investor-news/press-release-details/2020/Facebook-Reports-Fourth-Quarter-and-Full-Year-2019-Results/default.aspx.

"Facebook Unveils Facebook Ads." Meta (website). November 6, 2007. https://about.fb.com/news/2007/11/facebook-unveils-facebook-ads/.

"Facebook's Sheryl Sandberg." *Forbes*. August 20, 2009. https://www.forbes.com/forbes/2009/0907/power-women-09-facebook-sheryl-sandberg.html?sh=3e8ec0963873.

Forsgren, Nicole, Jez Humble, and Gene Kim. *Accelerate: The Science of Lean Software and DevOps: Building and Scaling High Performing Technology Organizations*. Portland, OR: IT Revolution Press, 2018.

Fox, Justin. "How to Succeed in Business by Bundling—and Unbundling." *Harvard Business Review*. November 2, 2014. https://hbr.org/2014/06/how-to-succeed-in-business-by-bundling-and-unbundling.

Gibbs, Samuel. "Flickr Bought by SmugMug as Yahoo Breakup Begins." *The Guardian*. April 23, 2018. https://www.theguardian.com/technology/2018/apr/23/flickr-bought-by-smugmug-yahoo-breakup.

Giles, Martin. "Exclusive: Banking Giant Capital One Enters B2B Software Industry With Launch of New Business." *Forbes*. June 1, 2022. https://www.forbes.com/sites/martingiles/2022/06/01/capitsl-one-enters-b2b-software-industry/?sh=548229f2d6b1.

Gillen, Al, Arnal Dayaratna, Jevin Jensen, and Katie Norton. "VMware Explores Its Way into New Market Dynamics." IDC. September 6, 2022. https://www.idc.com/getdoc.jsp?containerId=lcUS49661222.

Google. "Our Approach to Search." Google (webpage). Accessed March 18, 2024. https://www.google.com/search/howsearchworks/our-approach/.

Gordijn, Jaap, and Hans Akkermans. "Designing and Evaluating E-Business Models." *Intelligent Systems*, IEEE 16 (2001): 11–17. https://ieeexplore.ieee.org/document/941353.

Gray, Jim. "A Conversation with Werner Vogels." *acmqueue* 4, no 4 (June 30, 2006). https://queue.acm.org/detail.cfm?id=1142065.

Hagel, John, III. "Out of the Box: Strategies for Achieving Profits Today and Growth Tomorrow through Web Services." JohnHagel.com (blog). Accessed March 8, 2024. https://www.johnhagel.com/outofthebox/.

Hagel, John, III. "Unbundling the Corporation." *Harvard Business Review*. August 1, 2014. https://hbr.org/1999/03/unbundling-the-corporation.

Harford, Tim. "Why Didn't Electricity Immediately Change Manufacturing?" BBC World Service. August 20, 2017. https://www.bbc.com/news/business-40673694.

Hawkins, Andrew J. "Uber Ends the Year in the Black for the First Time Ever." *The Verge*. February 8, 2024. https://www.theverge.com/2024/2/8/24065999/uber-earnings-profitable-year-net-income.

"Jeff Bezos at MIT Amazon - Earth's Most Customer-Centric Company." YouTube video, 1:21:54, posted by MIT Video Production, posted on April 13, 2018. https://www.youtube.com/watch?v=J2xGBlT0cqY.

"John Pemberton, Coca-Cola." Lemelson-MIT (website). Accessed on March 8, 2024. https://lemelson.mit.edu/resources/john-pemberton.

Kirkpatrick, David. "Facebook's Plan to Hook Up the World." *CNN Money*. May 29, 2007. https://money.cnn.com/2007/05/24/technology/facebook.fortune/.

Koetsier, John. "Flickr Founder Stewart Butterfield's New Slack Signed Up 8,000 Companies in 24 Hours." VentureBeat. August 15, 2013. https://venturebeat.com/business/flickr-founder-stewart-butterfields-new-slack-signed-up-8000-companies-in-24-hours/.

Kolakowski, Mark. "Slack IPO: What You Need to Know." Investopedia. June 20, 2019. https://www.investopedia.com/slack-ipo-need-to-know-4685622.

"Largest Automakers by Market Capitalization." CompaniesMarketCap (website). Accessed March 11, 2024. https://companiesmarketcap.com/automakers/largest-automakers-by-market-cap/.

Licklider, J. C. R. *Libraries of the Future*. Cambridge, MA: MIT Press, 1965.

McKinley, Dan. "Design for Continuous Experimentation." McFunley.com (website). Accessed on March 8, 2024. https://mcfunley.com/continuous-experimentation/.

McLarty, Matt. "The Emerging API Opportunity with Fara Ashiru Jituboh," API's Unplugged (podcast). Produced by Mulesoft. 2022. https://soundcloud.com/mulesoft/apis-unplugged -s2-e8-the-emerging-api-opportunity-with-fara-asihru-jituboh.

Metz, Cade. "How Yahoo Spawned Hadoop, the Future of Big Data." *Wired*. October 18, 2011. https://www.wired.com/2011/10/how-yahoo-spawned-hadoop/.

Milch, Randy. "Uber GC Sallee Yoo on Comfort Zones and Seizing New Opportunities." In-House Legal (podcast). February 16, 2017. https://legaltalknetwork.com/podcasts/in-house-legal /2017/02/uber-gc-salle-yoo-comfort-zones-seizing-new-opportunities/.

Miller, Ron, and Alex Wilhelm. "Salesforce Buys Slack in a $27.7B Megadeal." *TechCrunch*. December 3, 2020. https://TechCrunch.com/2020/12/01/salesforce-buys-slack/.

Murphy, Bill, Jr. "Want to Succeed in Life? Ask for Forgiveness, Not Permission." Inc.com. January 5, 2021. https://www.inc.com/bill-murphy-jr/9-words-to-live-by-its-always-better-to-beg -forgiven.

O'Reilly, Tim. "Amazon Web Services API." O'Reilly Network. July 18, 2002. https://web.archive.org/ web/20020802192606/http://www.oreillynet.com/pub/wlg/1707.

O'Reilly, Tim. "The Network Really Is the Computer." O'Reilly Network. June 8, 2000. https://web. archive.org/web/20020618063515/http://www.oreillynet.com/pub/a/network/2000/06/09/ java_keynote.html?page=1.

Parker, Geoffrey G., Marshall W. Van Alstyne, and Sangeet Paul Choudary. *Platform Revolution: How Networked Markets Are Transforming the Economy and How to Make Them Work for You.* New York: Norton & Company, 2017.

Payne, Kenneth Wilcox. "A $10,000,000 'Accident.'" *Popular Science Monthly*. August 1927. https:// books.google.ca/books?id=ICoDAAAAMBAJ&q=%22Marvin+Pipkin%22+awarded +the+Charles+A.+Coffin+award&pg=PA24&redir_esc=y#v=snippet&q=%22Marvin%20 Pipkin%22%20awarded%20the%20Charles%20A.%20Coffin%20award&f=false.

Perez, Juan Carlos. "Yahoo Opens Up Web Mail APIs." *ComputerWorld*. March 29, 2007. https:// www.computerworld.com/article/2817862/yahoo-opens-up-web-mail-apis.html.

"Peter Senge." Vanguard: Beyond Command and Control (website). Accessed March 8, 2024. https:// beyondcommandandcontrol.com/library/whos-who-system-thinkers/peter-senge/.

Roof, Katie, and Liana Baker. "Goldman-Backed Startup Optimizely to Be Bought by Episerver." Bloomberg. September 3, 2020. https://www.bloomberg.com/news/articles/2020-09-03/ goldman-backed-startup-optimizely-to-be-acquired-by-episerver.

Scott, Kevin. "When Your Teach Debt Comes Due." LinkedIn article. July 20, 2017. https://www. linkedin.com/pulse/when-your-tech-debt-comes-due-kevin-scott/.

SE Daily. "Engineering Transformation at Scale with Chris Dillon." Software Engineering Daily. August 31, 2023. https://softwareengineeringdaily.com/2023/08/31/engineering -transformation/.

Shrivastava, Rashi. "LaunchDarkly Raises $200 Million, Hits $3 Billion Valuation to Prevent Technical Catastrophes." *Forbes*. Augsut 10, 2021. https://www.forbes.com/sites/rashishrivastava /2021/08/10/launchdarkly-raises-200-million-at-3-billion-valuation/?sh=14db2ba24381.

Son, Hugh. "Here's Why Capital One Is Buying Discover in the Biggest Proposed Merger of 2024." CNBC. February 21, 2024. https://www.cnbc.com/2024/02/21/why-capital-one-is-buying- discover-in-the-biggest-merger-yet-of-2024.html.

Statista. "Distribution of Unbanked Population 2011-2021, by Region," Statista (website). August 7, 2023. https://www.statista.com/statistics/553180/distribution-of-unbanked-population by -region/.

"Steve-Yegge-Google-Platform-Rant." Gist.Github.com. Posted by Kislayverma. Posted 2019. https://gist.github.com/kislayverma/d48b84db1ac5d737715e8319bd4dd368.

"Stevey's Google Platforms Rant." Gist.Github.com. Posted by Chitchcock. Accessed March 8, 2024. https://gist.github.com/chitchcock/1281611.

Taleb, Nassim Nicholas. *Antifragile: Things That Gain from Disorder*. New York: Random House, 2014.

Taleb, Nassim Nicholas. "Understanding Is a Poor Substitute for Convexity (Antifragility)." Edge. December 12, 2012. https://www.edge.org/conversation/nassim_nicholas_taleb-understanding -is-a-poor-substitute -for-convexity-antifragility.

Taylor, Bret. "The World Is Your JavaScript-Enabled Oyster." Google (blog). June 29, 2005. https://googleblog.blogspot.com/2005/06/world-is-your-javascript-enabled_29.html.

"Uber (UBER)—Market Capitalization." CompaniesMarketCap.com. Accessed March 11, 2024. https://companiesmarketcap.com/uber/marketcap/.

University of Virginia Press. "Founders Online: Advice to a Young Tradesman, [21 July 1748]," n.d. https://founders.archives.gov/documents/Franklin/01-03-02-0130.

Upbin, Bruce. "Salesforce to Buy ExactTarget for $2.5 Billion." *Forbes*. June 4, 2013. https://www.forbes.com/sites/bruceupbin/2013/06/04/salesforce-to-buy-exacttarget-for-2-5-billion/?sh=197a1a74cfcc.

Vlahovic, Tanya. "Celebrating 20 Years: eBay's New APIs Enable Developers to Create Modern Buying and Selling Experiences." eBay Tech Blog. July 13, 2020. https://innovation.ebayinc.com/tech/engineering/celebrating-20-years-ebays-new-apis-enable-developers-to-create-modern -buying-and-selling-experiences/.

Zara, Christopher. "How Facebook's 'Like' Button Hijacked Our Attention and Broke the 2010's." Fast Company. December 18, 2019. https://www.fastcompany.com/90443108/how-facebooks -like-button-hijacked-our-attention-and-broke-the-2010s.

Notes

Introduction

1. Arrington, "Facebook Launches Facebook Platform."
2. Christensen, *The Innovator's Dilemma*, 296.

Chapter 1

1. Harford, "Why Didn't Electricity Immediately Change Manufacturing?"
2. Harford, "Why Didn't Electricity Immediately Change Manufacturing?"
3. Bell, "Google Engineer Steve Yegge Has His Jerry Maguire Moment."
4. "Steve-Yegge-Google-Platform-Rant."
5. Bell, "Google Engineer Steve Yegge Has His Jerry Maguire Moment."
6. "Steve-Yegge-Google-Platform-Rant."
7. "Steve-Yegge-Google-Platform-Rant."
8. "Steve-Yegge-Google-Platform-Rant."
9. "Steve-Yegge-Google-Platform-Rant."
10. "Steve-Yegge-Google-Platform-Rant."
11. O'Reilly, "The Network Really Is the Computer."
12. O'Reilly, "Amazon Web Services API."
13. O'Reilly, "Amazon Web Services API."
14. O'Reilly, "Amazon Web Services API."
15. O'Reilly, "Amazon Web Services API."
16. O'Reilly, "Amazon Web Services API."
17. Christensen and Jassy, "60. Overcoming the Capitalist's Dilemma."
18. Christensen and Jassy, "60. Overcoming the Capitalist's Dilemma."
19. Christensen and Jassy, "60. Overcoming the Capitalist's Dilemma."
20. Christensen and Jassy, "60. Overcoming the Capitalist's Dilemma."
21. Google, "Our Approach to Search."
22. Taylor, "The World Is Your JavaScript-Enabled Oyster."
23. Interview with Thor Mitchell, February 2022.
24. Doyle, "Official Google Maps API Blog: Google Maps for Enterprise."
25. Interview with Thor Mitchell, February 2022.
26. Interview with Thor Mitchell, February 2022.

Chapter 2

1. "John Pemberton, Coca-Cola."
2. Crosby, "One Man's Force of Will Built a Retailing Empire."

3. Koetsier, "Flickr Founder Stewart Butterfield's New Slack Signed Up 8,000 Companies in 24 Hours."

4. Licklider, *Libraries of the Future*, 17.

5. "Business Model Canvas."

6. Interview with Geoff McCormack, March 2022.

7. Interview with Geoff McCormack, March 2022.

Chapter 3

1. Baldwin and Woodard, *The Architecture of Platforms*, 19–20.

2. Appleyard, "Books That Helped to Change The World."

3. Taleb, "Understanding Is a Poor Substitute for Convexity (Antifragility)."

4. Baldwin and Woodard, *The Architecture of Platforms*, 18–19.

5. Taleb, "Understanding Is a Poor Substitute for Convexity (Antifragility)."

6. "Amazon Web Services Launches."

7. Taleb, *Antifragile*, 182.

8. Taleb, "Understanding Is a Poor Substitute for Convexity (Antifragility)."

9. Taleb, *Antifragile*, 181.

10. Taleb, "Understanding Is a Poor Substitute for Convexity (Antifragility)."

11. Taleb, "Understanding Is a Poor Substitute for Convexity (Antifragility)."

12. Bell, "Google Engineer Steve Yegge Has His Jerry Maguire Moment."

13. Interview with Esat Sezer, February 2022.

14. Baldwin and Woodard, *The Architecture of Platforms*, 21.

15. Baldwin and Woodard, *The Architecture of Platforms*, 21.

16. Baldwin and Woodard, *The Architecture of Platforms*, 21.

17. Baldwin and Woodard, *The Architecture of Platforms*, 21.

18. Taleb, *Antifragile*, 180.

Chapter 4

1. "Business Model Canvas."

2. "Facebook Reports Fourth Quarter and Full Year 2019 Results."

3. The Associated Press, "Number of Active Users at Facebook Over the Years."

4. "Facebook's Sheryl Sandberg."

5. "Facebook's Sheryl Sandberg."

6. Dixon, "Annual Revenue and Net Income Generated by Meta Platforms from 2007 to 2023."

7. Drucker, "The Theory of the Business."

8. Christensen, *The Innovator's Dilemma*, 296.

9. Gordijn and Akkermans, "Designing and Evaluating E-Business Models."

10. Kirkpatrick, "Facebook's Plan to Hook Up the World."

11. "Facebook Unveils Facebook Ads."

12. Zara, "How Facebook's 'Like' Button Hijacked Our Attention and Broke the 2010's."

13. Arrington, "Facebook to Release a 'Like' Button for the Whole Darn Internet."

Chapter 5

1. Payne, "A $10,000,000 'Accident.'"

2. Payne, "A $10,000,000 'Accident.'"

3. "Jeff Bezos at MIT Amazon - Earth's Most Customer-Centric Company."

4. "Peter Senge."

5. McKinley, "Design for Continuous Experimentation."

Chapter 6

1. "Auto Innovators: New Data on Auto Industry's Economic Impact."

2. Gray, "A Conversation with Werner Vogels."

3. Gray, "A Conversation with Werner Vogels."

4. Gray, "A Conversation with Werner Vogels."

5. Carlier, "U.S. New and Used Car Sales 2010-2022."

6. SE Daily, "Engineering Transformation at Scale with Chris Dillon."

7. Interview with David Rice, February 11, 2022.

8. Interview with David Rice, February 11, 2022.

9. Conway, "How Do Committees Invent."

10. Interview with David Rice, February 11, 2022.

11. Interview with David Rice, February 11, 2022.

12. Interview with David Rice, February 11, 2022.

13. Interview with David Rice, February 11, 2022.

14. Interview with David Rice, February 11, 2022.

15. Scott, "When Your Teach Debt Comes Due."

16. Interview with David Rice, February 11, 2022.

17. Interview with David Rice, February 11, 2022.

18. Interview with David Rice, February 11, 2022.

19. Interview with David Rice, February 11, 2022.

20. Interview with Steve Stone, March 7, 2022.

21. Interview with Steve Stone, March 7, 2022.

22. Interview with Steve Stone, March 7, 2022.

23. Interview with Steve Stone, March 7, 2022.

24. Interview with Steve Stone, March 7, 2022.

25. Interview with Steve Stone, March 7, 2022.

26. Interview with Steve Stone, March 7, 2022.

27. Interview with Steve Stone, March 7, 2022.

28. Interview with Steve Stone, March 7, 2022.

29. Interview with Steve Stone, March 7, 2022.

30. Interview with Steve Stone, March 7, 2022.

31. Interview with Steve Stone, March 7, 2022.

Chapter 7

1. Gillen et al., "VMware Explores Its Way into New Market Dynamics."

2. Castle, "Who Are Knowledge Workers and How Do We Enable Them?"

3. O'Reilly, "Amazon Web Services API."

4. Vlahovic, "Celebrating 20 Years."

5. "Amazon Web Services - Adam Selipsky at USI."

6. "Steve-Yegge-Google-Platform-Rant."

7. Interview with Esat Sezer, February 2022.

8. Interview with Esat Sezer, February 2022.

9. Interview with Esat Sezer, February 2022.

10. Interview with Esat Sezer, February 2022.

11. Interview with Esat Sezer, February 2022.
12. Interview with Esat Sezer, February 2022.
13. Interview with Esat Sezer, February 2022.
14. Interview with Esat Sezer, February 2022.
15. Interview with Esat Sezer, February 2022.
16. "A Transformational Legacy."
17. Interview with Brian Scwheen and Denny Pichardo, December 2022.
18. Interview with Brian Scwheen and Denny Pichardo, December 2022.
19. Interview with Brian Scwheen and Denny Pichardo, December 2022.
20. Interview with Brian Scwheen and Denny Pichardo, December 2022.
21. Interview with Brian Scwheen and Denny Pichardo, December 2022.
22. Interview with Brian Scwheen and Denny Pichardo, December 2022.
23. Interview with Brian Scwheen and Denny Pichardo, December 2022.
24. Interview with Brian Scwheen and Denny Pichardo, December 2022.
25. Interview with Brian Scwheen and Denny Pichardo, December 2022.
26. Interview with Brian Scwheen and Denny Pichardo, December 2022.
27. Interview with Brian Scwheen and Denny Pichardo, December 2022.
28. Interview with Brian Scwheen and Denny Pichardo, December 2022.
29. Interview with Brian Scwheen and Denny Pichardo, December 2022.
30. Interview with Brian Scwheen and Denny Pichardo, December 2022.
31. Forsgren, Humble, and Kim, *Accelerate*, 47–48.

Chapter 8

1. Collins and Hansen, "How to Manage Through Chaos."
2. Collins, "Return on Luck."
3. Barr, "We Build Muck, So You Don't Have To."
4. Barr, "We Build Muck, So You Don't Have To."
5. Metz, "How Yahoo Spawned Hadoop, the Future of Big Data."
6. Perez, "Yahoo Opens Up Web Mail APIs."
7. Interview with Saurabh Sahni, March 4, 2022.
8. Interview with Saurabh Sahni, March 4, 2022.
9. Interview with Saurabh Sahni, March 4, 2022.
10. Interview with Saurabh Sahni, March 4, 2022.
11. Curry, "Slack Revenue and Usage Statistics (2024)."
12. Interview with Saurabh Sahni, March 4, 2022.
13. Interview with Saurabh Sahni, March 4, 2022.
14. Interview with Saurabh Sahni, March 4, 2022.
15. Interview with Saurabh Sahni, March 4, 2022.
16. Interview with Saurabh Sahni, March 4, 2022.
17. Interview with Saurabh Sahni, March 4, 2022.
18. Interview with Saurabh Sahni, March 4, 2022.
19. Interview with Saurabh Sahni, March 4, 2022.
20. Gibbs, "Flickr Bought by SmugMug as Yahoo Breakup Begins."
21. Kolakowski, "Slack IPO: What You Need to Know."
22. Miller and Wilhelm, "Salesforce Buys Slack in a $27.7B Megadeal."
23. DevExchange, Capital One, "Behind the Scenes at Capital One DevExchange—Capital One Tech —Medium."
24. Andrzejek, "Becoming a Fintech: Capital One's Move From Mainframes to the Cloud."

25. "Steve-Yegge-Google-Platform-Rant."
26. Giles, "Exclusive: Banking Giant Capital One Enters B2B Software Industry."
27. Giles, "Exclusive: Banking Giant Capital One Enters B2B Software Industry."
28. Giles, "Exclusive: Banking Giant Capital One Enters B2B Software Industry."
29. Giles, "Exclusive: Banking Giant Capital One Enters B2B Software Industry."
30. Son, "Here's Why Capital One Is Buying Discover in the Biggest Proposed Merger of 2024."
31. Roof and Baker, "Goldman-Backed Startup Optimizely to Be Bought by Episerver."
32. Shrivastava, "LaunchDarkly Raises $200 Million."
33. Upbin, "Salesforce to Buy ExactTarget for $2.5 Billion."

Chapter 9

1. Best Buy. *Best Buy Co., Inc. Fiscal 2000 Annual Report.*
2. Interview with Ian Kelly, March 2022.
3. Interview with Ian Kelly, March 2022.
4. Interview with Ian Kelly, March 2022.

Chapter 10

1. "Steve-Yegge-Google-Platform-Rant."
2. Hagel, "Unbundling the Corporation."; Hagel, "Out of the Box."
3. Parker, Van Alstyne, and Choudary, *Platform Revolution.*
4. Benzell et al., "How APIs Create Growth by Inverting the Firm."
5. Benzell et al., "How APIs Create Growth by Inverting the Firm"
6. Fox, "How to Succeed in Business by Bundling – and Unbundling."
7. Andreessen, "Yo."
8. Statista, "Distribution of Unbanked Population 2011-2021, by Region."
9. McLarty, "The Emerging API Opportunity with Fara Ashiru Jituboh."
10. Benzell et al., "How APIs Create Growth by Inverting the Firm."
11. Interview with Sanjna Verma, March 17, 2022.
12. Milch, "Uber GC Sallee Yoo on Comfort Zones and Seizing New Opportunities."
13. Murphy, "Want to Succeed in Life? Ask for Forgiveness, Not Permission."
14. "Stevey's Google Platforms Rant."
15. Fox, "How to Succeed in Business by Bundling – and Unbundling."
16. "Largest Automakers by Market Capitalization."; "Uber (UBER) - Market Capitalization."
17. "Largest Automakers by Market Capitalization."; "Uber (UBER) - Market Capitalization."
18. University of Virginia Press, "Founders Online: Advice to a Young Tradesman."
19. Hawkins, "Uber Ends the Year in the Black for the First Time Ever."

Chapter 11

1. Benzell et al., "How APIs Create Growth by Inverting the Firm."
2. Berners-Lee, *Weaving the Web*, 157–158.

Conclusion

1. Akamai, "Retail Attacks and API Traffic."

Acknowledgments

First and foremost, we want to offer our sincere thanks and gratitude to the digital leaders who made time in their hectic schedules to talk with us about their experiences and insights. We never wanted to write a book that was effectively us pontificating from on high about our perspectives on APIs and digital transformation. From the beginning, we had the aim to engage leaders from around the globe and across multiple industries both to identify the biggest obstacles to creating value and to get at the root of what works in successful transformations. Without the time, engagement, and amazing insights from our interviewees, we would not have been able to create this work.

While most of the interviewees are credited in the book, some do not have full sections dedicated to their stories and insights. Our genuine thanks go out to Jason Beyer, Lorinda Brandon, John D'Emic, Darren Goodson, James Higginbotham, Fara Ashiru Jituboh, Mia Jordan, Ian Kelly, Kevin Matheny, Geoff McCormack, Thor Mitchell, Ronnie Mitra, Mark O'Neill, Denny Pichardo, David Rice, Saurabh Sahni, Brian Schween, Esat Sezer, Steve Stone, and Sanjna Verma.

As this book is not only an output of the interviews but also a product of the life and work experiences we've had in our educational and professional careers, there are thousands of people who've helped us along the way to get to the point where we're now qualified to write this book. Parents, teachers, mentors, managers, peers, colleagues, friends, and staff we've had the privilege to lead have all contributed to making us the professionals we are today. Without a vibrant community with which to engage, we would not have been able to create this work.

We'd also like to thank Gene Kim; our editors, Anna Noak and Leah Brown; and the staff at IT Revolution for the support they gave and the belief they had in helping us develop and publish this work.

Last, without question, our spouses, Kathleen Kelly and Chris Cochran, not only created the space for us to develop this work but also supported us through decades of professional work and development. While neither of them may have helped build our technical acumen, more importantly they helped to form and temper our curious nature and apply it in the context of teams from where real innovation and insight springs.

About the Authors

Stephen Fishman (Fish) is the global practice lead for MuleSoft's success architect practice. He is a practicing technologist who brings creativity, rigor, and a human-centric lens to problem-solving. Known as an expert in aligning technology and business strategy, Stephen places a premium on pushing business and technology leaders to embrace iteration and the critical need to collaborate across disciplines. Throughout his career, Stephen has consulted with organizations desiring to transform their technology-based offerings to better meet the needs of organizations and the people they serve. In addition to consulting with large organizations, Stephen is an in-demand speaker and adviser. Stephen has worked in retail, healthcare, financial services, consumer goods, travel, government, and the nonprofit sector with a wide variety of global organizations to mature their technology and design capabilities. He lives in Atlanta with his family and when he's not working can be found biking on the many trails in Georgia.

Matt McLarty is the chief technology officer for Boomi. He works with organizations around the world to help them digitally transform using a composable approach. He is an active member of the global API community; has led global technical teams at Salesforce, IBM, and CA Technologies; and started his career in financial technology. Matt is an internationally known expert on APIs, microservices, and integration. He is coauthor of the O'Reilly books *Microservice Architecture* and *Securing Microservice APIs* and cohost of the API Experience podcast. He lives with his wife and two sons in Vancouver, BC.

How to Contact Us

Both Matt and Stephen are excited and eager to be of service to curious practitioners and leaders from every sector of business and public service. We're relentless problem solvers and would be happy to hear feedback from anyone who's interested to engage in positive dialogue with us. If you want to reach out, feel free to drop us a line via LinkedIn (www.linkedin.com/in/mattmclartybc/, www.linkedin.com/in/stephenhfishman/), or through our publisher, IT Revolution (itrevolution.com/).